THE *DAILY EXPRESS*
ENTERTAINING IN A FLASH

Beverley Piper is a freelance home economist who started writing about microwave cookery when working as a microwave oven demonstrator; she also presented a BBC series on microwave cookery. She originates recipes for various companies and often presents food for display, demonstrations and photography. She is the author of *Fast and Healthy Family Cooking*, *Beverley Piper's Quick and Easy Healthy Cookery* and *Super Juice* (Headline, 1993).

Beverley Piper is married to Malcolm Jarvis and they live in Kent.

GW00630885

The *Daily Express*
Entertaining
in a Flash

Beverley Piper

Illustrations by
Mike Gordon

HEADLINE

Copyright © text 1994 Beverley Piper
Copyright © illustrations 1994 Mike Gordon

The right of Beverley Piper to be identified as the
author of the Work has been asserted by her in accordance
with the Copyright, Designs and Patents Act 1988.

First published in 1994
by HEADLINE BOOK PUBLISHING

10 9 8 7 6 5 4 3 2 1

ISBN 0 7472 4361 1

Typeset by
Letterpart Limited, Reigate, Surrey

Printed and bound in Great Britain by
HarperCollins Manufacturing, Glasgow

HEADLINE BOOK PUBLISHING
A division of Hodder Headline PLC
338 Euston Road
London NW1 3BH

Contents

Acknowledgements

Grateful thanks to Tina Dorman for her help and support.

Thanks also to Holly Jarvis for helping me test recipes, even though the sun was shining one bright summer's day, and to Maddalena Bastianelli for her speedy work under pressure.

Thanks to Billingtons for supplying sugar; Gordon Winterbottom at Saphir Produce Ltd; Pillsbury Marketing; Alison Jee at Vital PR; The National Dried Fruit Trade Association (UK) Ltd; and Wally Hollands at Beoco Ltd.

Finally, I thank friends and family who tasted recipes as I tested, even when some formed a rather unusual meal!

Author's Note

---

* British standard measuring spoons, level, have been used throughout. These are available from most kitchen shops.

* Recipes are given in both imperial and metric weights. Don't mix weights.

* Where cartons, packets and tins are used, sizes printed on the actual products are used. Use the nearest size available.

* You will notice that when cooking rice in this book, both the rice and liquid are measured in the same measuring jug. For perfect results, always use this foolproof method.

Introduction

For hassle-free entertaining, everyone needs uncomplicated recipes that can be put together quickly, look impressive, taste delicious and work every time. The recipes in this book meet all these criteria. They are among my personal favourites and have been used for entertaining on many different occasions.

The book is divided into two main parts. The first part is designed to be used like any conventional cookbook, allowing you to sit down and relax with a glass of wine or a cup of coffee, whilst you flick through the sections and plan your meal.

There are plenty of imaginative starters, both hot and cold, including some light fruity ideas, interesting dips and unusual soups, such as Speedy Thai Soup (see page 240).

The main courses cover a wide range of foods, including recipes for vegetarians and delicious dishes for 'al fresco' eating during hot summer months, as well as plenty of interesting winter warmers too. Imagine Mustardy Mussels (see page 116) with chunks of warm granary bread to mop up the juices, or a delicate slice of Ham and Apricot Terrine (see page 100), with a Broad Bean and Sun-dried Tomato Salad (see page 259).

The vegetable and salad dishes are pretty to look at and crunchy and delicious to eat. You'll find friends eagerly tucking into second helpings as soon as they're offered. With plenty to choose from, enjoy selecting a light crisp salad or a hot vegetable stir-fry or purée to enhance and complement your main course.

The dessert section offers something for everyone, from simple ice cream ideas, to the more sophisticated recipe for Chestnut Purée with Raspberries (see page 140). There are a few wickedly sinful desserts as well as more healthy ones, too. Many of the puds follow a fruity theme as there really is nothing that quite comes up to the flavour and colour of fresh, ripe fruits. Never be afraid simply to serve a basket of top quality, fresh fruits instead of a dessert. What could be more simple or delicious than a perfectly ripe nectarine, peach or pear, or indeed a ripe British Cox's orange pippin. Most people still like to offer a cheese board with a selection of cheeses, but fresh fruits make an interesting, popular and healthy alternative.

The second part of the book gives a number of selected menus. Each has its own helpful time plan and is designed for a specific occasion for varying numbers of people. Designed to remove the headache and worry from your next party, you're sure to find this section useful and will come back to the menus time and time again.

THE ART OF PLANNING THE OCCASION

Careful advance organisation will make all the difference to your party, be it Sunday brunch for a few friends or a formal dinner for six business associates. Sit down in a relaxed atmosphere, with plenty of time and a pen and paper. Plan exactly the kind of party you want to give, considering space, cost, time available to produce food, china and glasses available, and so on. For large buffets and drinks parties, you will need help and space. Don't aim to cope with more than ten guests on your own. If at all possible, prepare some foods in advance as this will prove a real boon on the day of the party. However, remember to check you have adequate space available in the freezer or refrigerator.

THE MENU
Either select a menu from the back of the book and make a detailed shopping list from it, or select your own menu from the recipes in the first part of the book. Write the menu down, then make your shopping list and stick to it. Remember, the simpler the better. It's far more sensible to spend time with your guests in a relaxed atmosphere and serve mostly cold dishes, than to appear flustered and frightened with a cordon bleu menu that keeps you busy in the kitchen for most of the evening! Try to choose a balanced meal – don't select recipes that have eggs or cream in every course, and don't feel that you must always serve three courses. I often serve drinks with a few nibbles (the Spiced Cocktail Nuts [see page 46] and the Dates with Bacon [see page 45] would be ideal) in the lounge, followed by a two-course meal in the dining room or kitchen. A choice of desserts is nice, but ensure that one is made well in advance and only needs decorating before being served.

EQUIPMENT
Make good use of time-saving equipment to ease the work load when entertaining.

Microwave ovens
A boon for the cook in a hurry. You'll find several of the recipes give alternative instructions for microwave oven users. All have been tested on a microwave with an output of 700W, so remember you will have to increase timings slightly if your oven output is less than 700W.

Tips

- Use microwave ovens for re-heating cooked food to avoid it drying out. Even cooked rice and pasta re-heat to perfection.
- Butter and margarine can be softened for easy mixing and spreading. 225g (8oz) butter straight from the fridge takes about 1½ minutes to soften.
- Citrus fruits yield far more juice if popped in the microwave for a minute or so first. Two large lemons take about 1 minute on 100%/FULL power.

- Melt chocolate and dissolve soaked gelatine quickly and simply on SIMMER in the microwave.

Citrus zesters

To remove the zest quickly and easily from citrus fruits, invest in a zester. This little gadget, about the size of a potato peeler, is available in all good kitchen shops and is far easier to use and clean than a grater.

Electric hand-held mixers

For speedy creaming, beating or whipping, these machines are ideal. They are quick to assemble, and easy on the washing up too. Whip cream in a large jug to prevent splashing. Excellent for whisking mixtures, such as sponges, over a pan of hot water.

Food processors

These table-top machines really are like having a spare pair of hands in the kitchen. Where would the would-be hostess/host (who also cooks the meal) be without one? For chopping, shredding, dicing, blending, mixing, making mayonnaise, etc., they really are invaluable. Buy the largest size available – you'll only regret purchasing a smaller size that takes up as much space on the worktop anyway.

Always process dry ingredients first, progressing to wet mixtures at the end of your preparation. This way, with a bit of luck, you'll only have to wash the machine once, at the end.

Dishwashers

When entertaining, dishwashers are a boon. It is truly wonderful to have a cupboard where one can hide dirty dishes when time runs out and guests arrive early! Even though dishwashers probably will not cope with all the dirty crocks from a party, they do cope with the bulk of them. I really enjoy loading mine quickly after a dinner party and then going up to bed while the machine does the work.

HINTS AND TIPS

1. For dips in a flash, try serving a flavoured mayonnaise, or

keep Greek natural yoghurt and creamy fromage frais in the fridge. They can be blended with a little dried packet asparagus soup, curry paste, tomato purée with herbs, mashed avocado, anchovy sauce or smoked mackerel for instant dips. Apple slices dipped in lemon juice, sliced red pepper, carrot and celery sticks make instant healthy dunks alongside crisps and bread sticks.

2. For speedy, succulent grills, slash the flesh of meats, such as chicken, and fish, such as salmon and trout, fairly deeply in two or three places. This helps them to cook more quickly and prevents them from drying out. Always pre-heat the grill before cooking food, for sealed-in flavour.

3. Select a well balanced menu with dishes that complement each other. A light fruity starter would work well before steak or duck. Serve plenty of healthy fruits and crunchy veg for colour, flavour and texture.

4. Keep your eyes open in the supermarkets for new, labour-saving products, like sun-dried tomatoes, washed and pre-

pared salads, toasted flaked almonds, ground hazelnuts, meringue nests, etc. Keep a good stock of frozen and canned foods so that you can entertain quickly when friends drop in unexpectedly.

5. Freshly chopped parsley enhances so many dishes. Wash fresh parsley sprigs and shake dry. Seal in a polythene bag and store in the fridge for 3–4 days. Freeze sprigs of parsley for winter use. Crush frozen parsley to make instant chopped parsley.

6. Serve after-dinner coffee in small cups. The best coffee to use is freshly ground beans. Per person, allow about 25g (1oz) coffee per 300ml (10 fl oz) water. Never allow coffee to boil as this ruins the flavour. Make coffee in a filter or percolator, or if you have neither, use a jug. Simply put the required amount of medium ground coffee into a large jug. Pour on almost boiling water and leave to stand for 4–5 minutes, then strain the coffee either directly into cups or into a clean, warm jug. Serve a rich sweetmeat with coffee – baby meringues, Belgian chocolates, dates stuffed with marzipan, plump dried apricots dipped in melted chocolate and left to dry, or small macaroon biscuits are all ideal. If you can't be bothered with fresh coffee, a good quality instant, such as Nestlé Gold Blend, made according to instructions and kept in a thermos type jug for up to 1 hour, has an excellent flavour. Add cream or milk on serving.

7. Offer a variety of different types of cheese arranged on a board with celery and grapes and perhaps a few nuts in their shells. Remove the cheese from the fridge at least 1½ hours before the meal so that it realises its true flavour by the time you reach the cheese course. Leave it loosely wrapped until the last minute and serve with a variety of crackers in a basket, lined with a damask napkin. A reasonable selection of cheese would include one or two creamy varieties, such as a soft goats' cheese and perhaps *le Roule* cheese with garlic and herbs, one strong cheese such as Stilton and a couple of

milder flavoured cheeses such as English Cheddar and maybe a piece of Red Leicester. Cambazola, a soft German blue cheese, is always popular. Allow 50–75g (2–3oz) per person.

8. Arrange flowers well in advance. A small posy vase on the table is quite sufficient, perhaps with a larger vase wherever you wish to serve drinks. A terracotta vase filled with roses, lavender, poppies and some greenery provides a wonderful splash of colour and has the added bonus of a delicate perfume to fill the room, too.

9. Don't forget to organise pre-dinner drinks, glasses, nibbles and a stock of ice well in advance. It's very easy to forget when you are thinking about the meal, and some guests do arrive unfashionably early. As a basic guide offer gin (with tonic, ice and lemon), whisky (with soda or ginger ale), sherry (dry, medium and sweet), a good sparkling white wine, and plenty of fruit juices and mineral water. Ensure that cold drinks are well chilled, especially white wine, table water and fruit juices. Use a picnic coolbox when fridge space gets short.

10. Take the trouble to check whether your guests are vegetarian or vegan, have any food allergies or are on a strict diet. It saves the embarrassment of someone politely refusing to eat the main course!

11. Make good use of fresh herbs to enhance many dishes instantly. Tiny sprigs of variegated mint decorate desserts prettily, garnish savoury dishes and add flavour to salads. Basil, oregano, coriander, sage and parsley are all great on savoury dishes. Finely chopped herbs pep up sauces, soups, rice and pasta dishes.

12. For speed and ease, prepare salad leaves and vegetables early. Lettuce should be washed and well drained, then torn into bite-sized pieces, loosely sealed in plastic bags and placed in the fridge. Vegetables may be washed or

peeled and stored in sealed plastic bags in the fridge. Place prepared potatoes in cold water to which you have added a few drops of lemon juice. Cover with a lid and leave in the kitchen.

PART ONE

Starters

Tomato, Crab & Aubergine Soup
Serves 6

A true tomato flavour, this soup is excellent for dinner parties, yet so easy to make. If time allows, remove any bitter juices by placing the diced aubergine in a colander, sprinkle liberally with salt and set aside for 10 minutes. Rinse well under cold running water before using.

Preparation time: 5 mins
Cooking time: 22 mins

50g (2oz) butter
1 clove garlic, crushed
1 medium onion, chopped
175g (6oz) aubergine, diced
25g (1oz) plain flour
500ml (17 fl oz) passata
10ml (2 teaspoons) dried parsley
900ml (1¹/₂ pints) fish or chicken stock

150ml (5 fl oz) dry white wine or cider
Salt and freshly ground black pepper
10 frozen crab sticks, defrosted and shredded or *100g (4oz) white crab meat, flaked*

To serve
a few snipped chives or *50g (2oz) grated Gruyère cheese*

1. Melt the butter in a large, heavy-based pan.
2. Stir in the garlic and onion and sauté for about 5 minutes, until onion softens.
3. Stir in the aubergine and sauté for a further 5 minutes.
4. Stir in the flour and cook, stirring, for 1 minute.
5. Add the passata with the parsley, then gradually add the stock and the wine or cider, stirring continuously. Season.
6. Bring to the boil, stirring, then cover and simmer for 10 minutes.
7. Remove from the heat, stir in the crab. Check seasoning.

8. Ladle into individual soup bowls and serve garnished with a few snipped chives or sprinkled with grated Gruyère cheese.

Creamy Chick Pea & Chorizo Soup
Serves 6

A simple, yet well flavoured soup that is rich and creamy. Serve with warmed granary bread rolls.

Preparation time: 5 mins
Cooking time: 25 mins

25g (1oz) butter
1 large onion, finely chopped
1 × 430g (15oz) can chick peas
1 × 410g (14¹/₂oz) can
  evaporated milk

300ml (10 fl oz) vegetable
  stock
Freshly ground black pepper
350g (12oz) piece of chorizo
  sausage, thickly sliced

To serve
freshly chopped parsley

granary bread rolls

1. Melt the butter in a large, heavy-based pan.
2. Add the onion and sauté for 4–5 minutes, until lightly golden.
3. Meanwhile, purée the chick peas with their liquid in a food processor, then turn the purée into the pan with the onion. Gradually stir in the evaporated milk and the vegetable stock.
4. Bring to the boil, stirring, then cover and simmer for 10 minutes, stirring occasionally. Season to taste.
5. Add the sausage to the soup. Cover and simmer for a further 10 minutes.
6. Serve the soup, sprinkled with the chopped parsley.

Celery & Onion Soup au Gratin
Serves 6

An excellent party starter or snack lunch, this is similar to French onion soup with the added tang of celery. The brandy and Gruyère cheese make a quick and easy soup very special.

Preparation time: 5 mins
Cooking time: 34 mins

450g (1lb) onions
1/2 head celery
25g (1oz) butter
2 cloves garlic, crushed
30ml (2 tablespoons) plain flour

1.5 litres (21/2 pints) chicken, turkey or ham stock
150ml (5 fl oz) red wine
100g (4oz) Gruyère cheese
12 slices from a French loaf
30ml (2 tablespoons) brandy (optional)

1. Slice onions thinly, use the food processor if you have one, then chop celery.
2. Melt the butter in a large heavy saucepan or casserole dish. Add onions, garlic and celery and cook over a medium heat for 10 minutes, stirring now and again, until onions are soft and golden.
3. Stir in flour and cook for 1 minute, then pour in stock and wine. Simmer for 20 minutes, then remove lid and boil fast for 5 minutes. (You could prepare the soup to this stage in advance, if preferred.)
4. About 10 minutes before serving, pre-heat the grill, grate the cheese and make sure soup is simmering.
5. Arrange bread on grill rack. Top with grated cheese.
6. Grill until cheese is melted and golden and bread is toasted.
7. Stir brandy into soup, if using, then serve the soup in bowls, with bread floating, or let guests float their own – it's quicker!

Chilled Strawberry Soup
Serves 6

Fresh and fruity, this light starter is very pretty to serve. Good before a rich main course, it is important to serve this soup very cold, so prepare in advance and chill in the fridge for 20 minutes. This soup is also good for cleansing the palate between courses.

Preparation time: 5 mins
Cooking time: 0

450g (1lb) strawberries, washed and hulled
400ml (14 fl oz) unsweetened apple juice, chilled

60ml (4 tablespoons) extra thick double cream

To garnish
6 small strawberries

6 sprigs of fresh mint

1. Slice strawberries and place in food processor.
2. Add apple juice. Blend until smooth.
3. Add cream and blend again.
4. Pour into chilled, individual glass bowls and chill. Serve each bowl garnished with a strawberry and a sprig of mint.

Fettuccine with Smoked Ham & Cheese
Serves 6

This is an easy starter to prepare and serve at the last minute. Always cook pasta in a large pan of boiling water with a little oil added. Don't cover the pan and stir a few times during cooking to prevent the pasta from sticking. Fettuccine is a flat spaghetti, but if you find spaghetti too much of a hassle for guests to cope with, use pasta twists or shells instead, or perhaps campanelle (rolled trumpet-like shapes). Cook according to packet instructions.

Preparation time: 5 mins
Cooking time: 10 mins

450g (1lb) fettuccine
5ml (1 teaspoon) sunflower oil
25g (1oz) butter
1 medium onion, chopped
300ml (10 fl oz) double cream
10ml (2 teaspoons) granary mustard
60ml (4 tablespoons) dry white wine

Salt and freshly ground black pepper
175g (6oz) sliced smoked ham, cut into thin strips
30ml (2 tablespoons) freshly chopped parsley

To serve
grated Parmesan cheese

1. Cook the fettuccine in a large pan of boiling water, with the oil for 6–7 minutes until 'al dente' ('to the tooth'). Stir a couple of times to prevent sticking.
2. Meanwhile, melt the butter in a large saucepan. Add the onion and sauté for 5 minutes.
3. Add the cream, mustard and wine, whisk and heat to simmering point. Remove from heat. Season to taste with salt and pepper and stir in the ham and parsley.
4. Drain the fettuccine and turn into six warmed serving bowls. Top with cream mixture and serve immediately, handing the Parmesan round separately.

Pesto Noodles with Smoked Turkey
Serves 6

This is an elegant starter that takes no time to prepare and cook. Really good jars of pesto sauce are now readily available in leading supermarkets. Red pesto sauce has sun-dried tomatoes added, giving it a rich tomato flavour. Dried Chinese noodles are available from supermarkets.

Preparation time: 5 mins
Cooking time: 8 mins

350g (12oz) Chinese egg noodles
1 × 190g (6¹/₂oz) jar red pesto sauce

30ml (2 tablespoons) virgin olive oil
175g (6oz) smoked turkey or ham, roughly chopped

To garnish
fresh basil leaves or *Parmesan cheese*

1. Cook the noodles in a large pan of boiling water for 4 minutes, or according to the directions on the packet.
2. Drain noodles and return to pan.
3. Add the pesto sauce with the olive oil.
4. Toss everything together to mix well.
5. Serve in individual serving bowls, topped with the smoked turkey or ham, and garnished with the fresh basil leaves or a sprinkling of Parmesan cheese.

Quick Cheese & Asparagus Soufflés
Serves 6

These light, crisp soufflés have a good flavour and make an excellent starter on a cold winter's night. Serve with granary bread.

Preparation time: 10 mins
Cooking time: 15–20 mins

Butter, for greasing
1 × 310g (10¹/₂oz) can condensed asparagus soup
100g (4oz) Cheddar cheese, grated
30ml (2 tablespoons) grated Parmesan cheese

4 eggs, size 2, separated
Salt and freshly ground black pepper
About 15ml (1 tablespoon) grated Parmesan cheese

1. Pre-heat the oven to 375°F (190°C) gas mark 5.
2. Lightly grease six ramekin dishes with the butter.
3. Put the soup into a large non-stick pan and heat through gently, stirring, until warm.
4. Remove from heat and beat in the cheeses. Beat in egg yolks, one at a time. Season to taste.
5. Beat egg whites until stiff in a clean mixing bowl, with a clean whisk.
6. Beat 15ml (1 tablespoon) beaten egg white into the soup mixture, then fold in the remainder quickly and evenly, with a metal spoon.
7. Divide soufflé mixture between the ramekins. Dust with Parmesan cheese.
8. Bake for 15–20 minutes until well risen and golden. Serve immediately.

Bruschetta
Serves 6

Serve as a starter with a tossed mixed salad or on their own with pre-dinner nibbles. A popular Italian appetiser.

Preparation time: 10 mins
Cooking time: 4 mins

1 small French baguette, cut into 16 slices
Virgin olive oil
1 clove garlic, cut in half
30ml (2 tablespoons) pesto sauce

100g (4oz) mozzarella cheese, sliced
50g (2oz) pitted black olives, sliced
Basil leaves
1 mini le Roule *cheese with herbs and garlic*

1. Brush bread slices generously with olive oil and toast lightly under the grill on both sides.
2. Rub the toast with the cut clove of garlic.
3. Spread eight slices with the pesto sauce and top with the mozzarella and olives.
4. Grill for about 4 minutes, until cheese melts. Sprinkle with basil leaves and serve warm.
5. Meanwhile, cut the mini *le Roule* cheese into eight slices.
6. Top remaining croûtes with cheese and serve immediately.

Mushrooms en Cocotte
Serves 6

This delicious hot starter can be prepared in advance, then baked while your friends enjoy a pre-dinner drink.

Note: To make quick melba toast, lightly toast slices from a thick cut white loaf, on both sides, under the grill. Using a sharp knife and chopping board, cut each slice in half to give two full-size slices from each slice. Toast untoasted sides again until curled and browned.

Preparation time: 5 mins
Cooking time: 15 mins

Olive oil, for greasing
225g (8oz) mixed mushrooms,
* such as oyster, field and*
* morel if possible, or button*
50g (2oz) butter
Salt and freshly ground black
* pepper*

1 clove garlic, crushed
450ml (15 fl oz) double cream
45ml (3 tablespoons) grated
* Parmesan cheese*
Paprika pepper

To garnish
fresh parsley sprigs

To serve
melba toast

1. Pre-heat the oven to 375°F (190°C) gas mark 5.
2. Lightly oil six ramekin dishes and set on a baking sheet.
3. Slice mushrooms thickly and divide between ramekins.
4. Dot with the butter and season with a little salt and pepper.
5. Mix garlic into the cream, then pour cream over mushrooms.
6. Sprinkle with Parmesan cheese and dust with paprika pepper.
7. Bake for 10–15 minutes until golden.
8. Garnish with parsley sprigs and serve immediately with melba toast.

Bacon & Aubergine Frittata
Serves 6

This omelette-like starter is equally delicious served hot or cold. Use as a starter for six or an easy supper or lunch for four. If time allows, remove any bitter juices from the aubergine using the method described on page 11.

Preparation time: 10 mins
Cooking time: 15 mins

45ml (3 tablespoons) olive oil
225g (8oz) aubergine, diced
100g (4oz) lightly smoked streaky bacon, rinded and chopped
1 courgette, sliced
1 small onion, chopped

30ml (2 tablespoons) fresh herbs (thyme, parsley, chives), chopped
Salt and freshly ground black pepper
6 eggs, size 2
50g (2oz) cheese, grated

To serve
salad garnish

1. Heat the oil in a large 25.5cm (10in) frying pan.
2. Add the diced aubergine to the pan with the bacon, courgette and onion. Sauté for 4–5 minutes.
3. In a medium mixing bowl, whisk together the herbs, salt and pepper, eggs and 45ml (3 tablespoons) cold water. Use a fork or a balloon whisk.
4. Pour beaten eggs over the aubergine mixture and cook over a medium heat for 4–5 minutes, until set.
5. Pre-heat the grill to high.
6. Sprinkle grated cheese over frittata. Put the frying pan under the grill to brown top of the omelette.
7. Serve immediately, cut into wedges with a salad garnish, or serve cold, roughly chopped, with salad and a vinaigrette dressing.

Anchovy & Tomato Baked Eggs
Serves 6

These oven-baked eggs make a quick, substantial starter and are also good for a snack lunch, in which case you may like to serve two per person. A truly delicious way to serve eggs, the herbs are an important part of this dish. Serve with crusty French bread.

Note: To blanch tomatoes, put them into a mixing bowl and cover with boiling water. When skins 'split' after about a minute, drain off water and replace with cold water. The skins will peel off very easily.

Preparation time: 10 mins
Cooking time: 14–19 mins

15g (¹/₂oz) butter
3 medium-sized tomatoes, blanched
Salt and freshly ground black pepper
6 eggs, size 2 (free-range if possible)
1 × 50g (2oz) can anchovies
90ml (6 tablespoons) double cream

To serve
30ml (2 tablespoons) freshly chopped parsley, basil and chives

1. Pre-heat the oven to 375°F (190°C) gas mark 5.
2. Butter six cocotte or ramekin dishes with the butter.
3. Peel and chop the tomatoes, discarding seeds and divide between ramekins. Season with a little salt and pepper.
4. Carefully break one egg into each dish.
5. Drain anchovy strips on absorbent kitchen paper. Chop, then arrange over eggs, dividing them evenly. Stand dishes in a roasting tin.
6. Carefully pour enough boiling water into the roasting tin to come halfway up the ramekins. This is important, as insufficient water means the eggs will not set.
7. Place the roasting dish in the oven and bake for 10–15 minutes, until whites are just set.
8. Spoon a tablespoon of cream over each egg. Sprinkle with the herbs and return to the oven for a further 4 minutes. Serve immediately.

Moules Marinières
Serves 6

Mussels are ever popular and now available fresh in many supermarkets. Very simple to cook and serve, you just need an extra large pan to cook them in.

Preparation time: 15 mins
Cooking time: 5 mins

6lb (2.7kg) mussels
25g (1oz) butter
1 small onion, chopped
2 cloves garlic, finely chopped
15 ml (1 tablespoon) red wine vinegar

450ml (15 fl oz) dry white wine
60ml (4 tablespoons) freshly chopped parsley
Freshly ground black pepper

To serve
chunks of French bread

1. Scrub each mussel thoroughly and pull away the beard – this is the stubborn tuft by which the mussels cling to rocks.
2. Melt the butter in a very large pan. Add onion and garlic and sauté for 5 minutes.
3. Stir in the vinegar and wine with 30ml (2 tablespoons) of the chopped parsley.
4. Bring to the boil, then add the mussels. (Steam them in two batches if you can't get them all into the pan in one go.)
5. Shake the pan as the mussels open and cook – they will only take 2–3 minutes. Don't over-cook or they will be tough.
6. Transfer with a draining spoon to a large, warm serving bowl. Discard any mussels that do not open.
7. Boil cooking liquid hard to reduce a little, then season to taste. Strain liquid through a sieve over the mussels. Sprinkle with reserved parsley and serve immediately with plenty of French bread to mop up the delicious juices.

Prawn & Pesto Pancakes

Serves 6 (makes 12 mini pancakes)

Mini pancakes, quickly fried, then served with a creamy topping
and plump prawns – irresistible! Also good served warm spread
with the Tapenade on page 41, instead of the crème fraîche and
prawns.

Preparation time: 15 mins
Cooking time: 10 mins

For the pancakes

100g (4oz) self-raising flour
15ml (1 tablespoon) sunflower
oil
1.25ml (¼ teaspoon) salt
1 egg, size 2

15ml (1 tablespoon) red pesto
sauce
150ml (5 fl oz) milk
Oil, for frying

For the topping

15ml (1 tablespoon) freshly
chopped parsley
1 × 200ml (7 fl oz) carton
crème fraîche
Salt and freshly ground black
pepper

175g (6oz) large peeled
prawns, defrosted if frozen
12 tiny sprigs of mint or
parsley

1. Put the flour into a large mixing bowl. Make a well in centre
   and pour in oil, salt, egg, pesto sauce and milk.
2. Using a wooden spoon, gradually draw the dry ingredients
   into the liquid. Beat to make a smooth batter, then continue
   to beat for 2–3 minutes. Set aside for 5 minutes.
3. Meanwhile, prepare the filling. Stir chopped parsley into
   crème fraîche. Season lightly with salt and pepper.
4. Lightly grease a large, heavy-based frying pan with a little oil
   and place over a moderate heat until hot.
5. Drop dessertspoons of the mixture from the point of the
   spoon into the hot pan, keeping them well apart to allow for
   spreading. Cook for 2–3 minutes, until bubbling on the

surface. You should be able to cook about six pancakes at a time.

6. Turn with a palette knife and cook for a further 2–3 minutes, until golden brown.

7. Keep the pancakes warm by wrapping in a cloth while you cook remainder.

8. Serve two warm pancakes per person, topped with a spoonful of the crème fraîche mixture and the prawns and garnished with mint or parsley.

Crispy Stilton-topped Avocado with Prawns
Serves 4

A tasty hot starter which is very popular. For speed, make the topping in the food processor by processing the roughly torn bread with the cheese, then empty the machine and use again briefly to chop the avocado flesh.

Preparation time: 10 mins
Cooking time: 5 mins

2 large, ripe avocados
100g (4oz) peeled, cooked prawns, defrosted if frozen
75ml (5 tablespoons) fromage frais
5ml (1 teaspoon) tomato purée

1 clove garlic, crushed
Salt and freshly ground black pepper
2.5ml (1/2 teaspoon) lemon juice

For the topping

25g (1oz) fresh brown breadcrumbs

25g (1oz) Stilton cheese, grated

1. Halve the avocados and remove the central stone.
2. Scoop out flesh from each half, chop and place in mixing bowl. Reserve the avocado skins.
3. Pre-heat the grill to medium hot.
4. Roughly chop the prawns and add to the mixing bowl.
5. Add the fromage frais, tomato purée and the garlic. Mix well.
6. Season lightly with salt and pepper and stir in the lemon juice.
7. Pile the mixture back into avocado skins.
8. Combine breadcrumbs and cheese and sprinkle evenly over the filled avocados.
9. Place on grill rack and cook, watching carefully, until golden. Serve immediately.

Creamy Scrambled Eggs with Smoked Ham
Serves 6

Great for a quick, hot starter or lunchtime snack. Toasted muffins make a good alternative to bread.

Preparation time: 5 mins
Cooking time: 10 mins

8 eggs, size 2
90ml (6 tablespoons) single cream
Salt and freshly ground black pepper
25g (1oz) butter
3 wholemeal muffins
Low-fat spread or butter, for spreading
3 slices smoked ham, halved

To serve
freshly snipped chives

1. In a mixing bowl beat together the eggs and cream and season with salt and pepper.
2. Melt the butter in a medium-sized, non-stick saucepan. Pour in egg mixture and cook, stirring continuously, over a low heat until eggs are lightly scrambled.
3. Meanwhile, split and toast the muffins. Spread lightly with low-fat spread or butter.
4. To serve, place a half slice of smoked ham on each toasted muffin half. Top with the scrambled egg and sprinkle with a few freshly snipped chives. Serve immediately.

Dressed Seafood Salad
Serves 6

This refreshing salad is served with a warm lemon dressing which brings out the delicate flavour of the fish.

Preparation time: 15 mins
Cooking time: 6 mins

12 large cooked prawns
18 raw mussels, scrubbed
*   clean*

150ml (5 fl oz) dry white wine
6 raw oysters
350g (12oz) smoked trout fillet

For the dressing

5ml (1 teaspoon) red wine
*   vinegar*
120ml (4 fl oz) olive oil

Juice of 1/2 lemon
Sea salt and freshly ground
*   black pepper*

To serve
mixed salad leaf garnish

thyme, marjoram or chive
*   flowers*

1. Prepare the prawns – remove heads and peel off the shells, leaving tail ends on the prawns. Slice down the back of each prawn and remove the black vein.
2. Put mussels into a medium saucepan with the wine and bring to the boil. Cook, covered, over a fairly high heat for 2 minutes, until the shells open. Remove mussels with a draining spoon and set aside. Discard any mussels that have not opened.
3. Open the oyster shells with a blunt, round bladed knife. Leave oysters raw, but add any liquid from the shells to the stock.
4. Boil stock fairly rapidly until it reduces to 45ml (3 tablespoons).
5. Remove from heat and gradually whisk in the vinegar and the oil.

6. Whisk in lemon juice and season to taste with salt and pepper.
7. To serve, divide the mixed salad leaf garnish between six plates. Top with the seafood, arranging it attractively.
8. Garnish with the herb flowers and serve the warm dressing separately.

Tomato and Liver Pâté
with Mascarpone Cheese
Serves 6

A creamy pâté that can be prepared the day before, if preferred. One large tomato holds the perfect amount of pâté for one serving. Serve with a knife and fork so that guests can eat both the tomato shell and the pâté with the toast.

Preparation time: 15 mins
Cooking time: 15 mins + chilling time

6 fairly large English tomatoes
75g (3oz) butter
1 medium onion, finely chopped
350g (12oz) chicken livers, chopped, discarding any membrane

5ml (1 teaspoon) dried oregano
Salt and freshly ground black pepper
30ml (2 tablespoons) dry sherry
175g (6oz) Mascarpone cream cheese

To garnish
salad leaf garnish

wedges of lemon

To serve
wholemeal toast

1. Cut a slice from the top of each tomato. Scoop out the flesh from inside and reserve, discarding core and seeds. Turn tomatoes upside down to drain.
2. Melt the butter in a large frying pan and sauté the onion for 5 minutes until softened.
3. Add the liver and continue to sauté for 3–4 minutes, until lightly browned on all sides. The livers should still be pink in the centre.
4. Add the tomato pulp and the oregano and continue to cook for 3 minutes.

5. Remove from heat and season with a little salt and pepper.
6. Set aside for 5 minutes, then turn contents of the pan into the food processor. Add the sherry and process until smooth.
7. Add cheese and process until a smooth paste results.
8. Pipe or spoon the mixture into tomato shells.
9. Chill in refrigerator until ready to serve or for at least 20 minutes.
10. Serve the tomatoes on small plates with the salad leaf garnish and wedges of lemon, accompanied by wholemeal toast.

Crab-stuffed Mushrooms
Serves 6

These can be prepared up to 1 hour before the meal. Cover and chill in the fridge until ready to cook. Choose mushrooms of a similar size and serve with bread to mop up the juices.

Preparation time: 10 mins
Cooking time: 20 mins

18 medium-sized flat
   mushrooms
45ml (3 tablespoons) olive oil
2 rashers back bacon, rinded
   and chopped
1 small onion, finely chopped
1 clove garlic, crushed
30ml (2 tablespoons) freshly
   chopped parsley
10ml (2 teaspoons) lemon juice

75g (3oz) fresh brown
   breadcrumbs
8 crab sticks, defrosted if
   frozen, and chopped
15ml (1 tablespoon)
   mayonnaise
40g (1½oz) Cheddar cheese,
   grated
A little paprika pepper

1. Pre-heat the oven to 375°F (190°C) gas mark 5.
2. Carefully remove stalks from mushrooms. Place mushrooms on a greased baking tray and brush lightly with oil.
3. Heat remaining oil in a medium saucepan. Stir in bacon, onion and garlic, and sauté over a medium heat until onion softens and bacon starts to crisp.
4. Remove from heat and stir in all remaining ingredients except for cheese and paprika.
5. Stuff mushrooms with crab mixture. Sprinkle with grated cheese, then top each mushroom with a little paprika.
6. Bake for 12–15 minutes. Serve immediately.

Smoked Salmon Cornets
Serves 6

Light and delicious, these pretty smoked salmon starters may be prepared well in advance. Serve with thinly sliced brown bread and butter.

Preparation time: 10 mins
Cooking time: 0

225g (8oz) cream cheese, at room temperature
Grated rind of 1/2 orange
30ml (2 tablespoons) mayonnaise
60ml (4 tablespoons) freshly chopped dill

225g (8oz) peeled, cooked prawns, thoroughly defrosted and drained if frozen
6 large, thin slices smoked salmon
Freshly ground black pepper

To garnish
wedges of lemon   *coriander leaves*

1. Beat the cream cheese in a bowl with the orange rind and mayonnaise. Fold in the dill.
2. Roughly chop the prawns.
3. Spread a good tablespoon of the cheese mixture over each salmon slice. Sprinkle the chopped prawns over.
4. Roll each slice of salmon into a cornet shape and arrange on a serving dish. Season with a little black pepper. Serve with a wedge of lemon for squeezing over and a few coriander leaves.

Nectarines with Prawns
Serves 6

The slightly acidic sweetness of the nectarines combines well with the prawns and creamy mustard dressing. Serve with brown bread and butter.

Preparation time: 10 mins
Cooking time: 0

350g (12oz) large peeled
   prawns, defrosted if frozen
100g (4oz) mixed salad leaves

6 ripe nectarines
10ml (2 teaspoons) fresh
   tarragon

For the dressing

30ml (2 tablespoons)
   wholegrain mustard
75ml (5 tablespoons)
   mayonnaise

45ml (3 tablespoons) soured
   cream
Salt and freshly ground black
   pepper

1. Make the dressing. Place the mustard with the mayonnaise and soured cream in a mixing bowl. Stir to blend. Season to taste with salt and pepper.
2. Stir the prawns into the dressing to coat.
3. Just before serving, arrange the salad leaves on six medium-sized plates.
4. Halve the nectarines and remove the stones.
5. Slice the nectarines and arrange slices on each plate of salad.
6. Add a spoonful of prawns in dressing to each plate.
7. Sprinkle with tarragon and serve immediately.

Avocados with Walnut Vinaigrette
Serves 6

The avocados must be top quality for this starter. Choose the black, rough skinned ones if possible and ensure that there are no black spots amongst the green flesh if you buy smooth ones. Buy one or two extra avocados just in case.

Preparation time: 10 mins
Cooking time: 0

60ml (4 tablespoons) walnut oil
15ml (1 tablespoon) lime juice
Salt and freshly ground black pepper

3 large, ripe avocados
100g (4oz) walnut pieces, roughly chopped
30ml (2 tablespoons) freshly chopped dill

To serve
brown bread and butter

1. In a mixing bowl whisk together the walnut oil, lime juice and salt and pepper to taste.
2. Halve the avocados and remove the stones, then carefully peel each half.
3. Lay each peeled avocado half, flat side down, on a board. Cut evenly across into slices, then 'fan' the slices out gently. Transfer each fan to individual serving plates using a fish slice.
4. Spoon dressing over avocados immediately.
5. Sprinkle nuts over evenly, then add the dill.
6. Serve within 20 minutes to prevent discolouration, accompanied by the brown bread and butter.

Avocados with a Strawberry Coulis
Serves 6

This speedy starter with its pretty combination of colours will make any meal into an occasion.

Preparation time: 10 mins
Cooking time: 10–15 mins chilling

450g (1lb) ripe strawberries, roughly chopped
Juice of 1/2 lemon

Sieved icing sugar, to taste
3 large, ripe avocados

To serve
sprigs of mint

1. Make the strawberry sauce by blending the strawberries in the food processor, then sieving to make a purée.
2. Add the lemon juice and stir in just enough sugar to take the 'edge' off the sauce – it shouldn't taste sweet. Chill for 10–15 minutes; the sauce will thicken slightly.
3. Halve the avocados and remove the stones.
4. Carefully peel each avocado, then arrange them, flat side down, on six small plates.
5. Slice avocados like a fan, but do not cut right through narrow end. Gently push sliced avocados and they will naturally form fans.
6. Spoon some strawberry sauce onto each plate, beside the avocado fans and serve immediately, garnished with a sprig of mint.

Orange, Grapefruit & Cambozola Starter
Serves 6

A delicious combination of flavours that make a light, tasty starter. Serve with granary rolls or wholemeal toast.

Preparation time: 15 mins
Cooking time: 0

2 large oranges   *175g (6oz) Cambozola cheese*
1 large pink grapefruit

For the dressing

45ml (3 tablespoons) olive oil   *Freshly ground black pepper*
30ml (2 tablespoons) orange
   juice

To serve
sprigs of watercress   *30ml (2 tablespoons) sesame*
                      seeds, toasted

1. Remove the peel from one orange, being careful not to remove any pith. Cut into very thin strips and blanch in boiling water. Drain and set aside.
2. Peel remaining orange and the grapefruit, catching any drips and removing all pith and skin. Remove pith from first orange.
3. Segment oranges and grapefruit, removing membrane and pips. Slice the Cambozola fairly thinly.
4. Prepare the dressing. Combine any drips resulting from the fruit with the olive oil and orange juice. Whisk with a fork, adding a seasoning of black pepper.
5. Arrange the fruit segments and sliced Cambozola on six individual plates.
6. Drizzle dressing over, garnish with watercress sprigs and sprinkle with toasted sesame seeds. Serve immediately.

Gorgonzola Stuffed Pears
Serves 6

Gorgonzola is a rich, creamy, Italian blue cheese with a robust flavour. The combination of pears with cheese is wonderful.
Note: You may prefer not to peel the pears.

Preparation time: 15 mins
Cooking time: 0

6 ripe Williams pears
100g (4oz) reduced fat cream cheese
75g (3oz) Gorgonzola, grated

30–45ml (2–3 tablespoons) milk
Freshly ground black pepper

To serve
a few mixed salad leaves, shredded
30ml (2 tablespoons) olive oil

grated rind and juice of $^1/_2$ orange

1. Peel, halve and core the pears.
2. Put the cream cheese into a mixing bowl. Using a wooden spoon, beat in the Gorgonzola and the milk to form a soft consistency. Season with a little black pepper.
3. Put the mixed salad leaves into a bowl. Add the oil with the rind and juice of the orange. Toss to coat.
4. Arrange salad leaves on six small plates.
5. Spoon the cheese mixture into the hollows of the pears.
6. Arrange two stuffed pear halves on each plate and serve immediately.

Tapenade
Serves 6

Made rather like mayonnaise, in the blender, this fishy starter is delicious with warm rolls and a salad garnish. Many delicatessen counters now sell pitted black olives. If the anchovies are canned in olive oil, reserve it and use in the recipe.

Preparation time: 15 mins
Cooking time: 0

2 × 50g (2oz) can anchovy
   fillets with capers
45ml (3 tablespoons) milk
100g (4oz) pitted black olives
1 × 185g (6¹/₂oz) can tuna
   chunks in brine, drained

85ml (3 fl oz) virgin olive oil
Grated rind and juice of ¹/₂
   lemon
30ml (2 tablespoons) brandy
   or good dry sherry
Freshly ground black pepper

To serve
warm French bread or granary
   rolls

salad garnish
wedges of lemon

1. Drain the oil from the anchovies, then turn them into a bowl with the capers. Pour over the milk and set aside for 10 minutes while you get everything else ready. (This is so that the strong anchovy flavour isn't quite so pronounced.) Drain well. Discard the milk.
2. Put the anchovies and capers into the food processor with the olives and tuna fish. Process to a smooth paste.
3. Add the olive oil and lemon juice, drop by drop, using the drip feed if you have one, as though you are making mayonnaise. Process until a smooth, thick paste is formed. Stir in the lemon rind, brandy or sherry and the black pepper to taste. Turn into a small pâté dish. Chill until ready to serve.
4. Serve with warmed bread and a salad garnish, accompanied by wedges of lemon.

Fig & Walnut Starters
Serves 6

Everyone will enjoy this slightly different, light starter. Serve with warm rolls and butter.

Preparation time: 10 mins
Cooking time: 0

*1 bag ready prepared
    Continental leaves*
1 red skinned eating apple
1 green skinned eating apple

Juice of ¹/₂ orange
*3 fresh figs, sliced (or use
    dried)*
100g (4oz) walnut halves

For the dressing

*1 × 200g (7oz) carton crème
    fraîche*
5ml (1 teaspoon) clear honey
5ml (1 teaspoon) lemon juice

*15ml (1 tablespoon) freshly
    chopped coriander*
*Salt and freshly ground black
    pepper*

To garnish
wedges of orange

1. Prepare the dressing. Put the crème fraîche into a mixing bowl, add the honey, lemon juice, coriander and a seasoning of salt and pepper. Stir to blend.
2. Divide the salad leaves between six medium-sized plates, tearing them into smaller pieces if necessary.
3. Core and chop the apples roughly. Put them into a bowl and sprinkle over the orange juice. Toss to coat, then arrange apples on salad leaves. Add the figs.
4. Spoon the creamy dressing over the salads. Top with the walnuts and serve the salads immediately, garnished with wedges of orange.

Cheesy Garlic & Herb Bread
Serves 6

Delicious served on its own or with dishes of black and green olives and gherkins from the deli. Good with the Thai-style soup on page 240 too. For a change, try adding 15ml (1 tablespoon) wholegrain mustard with whisky to the butter.

Preparation time: 10 mins
Cooking time: 25–30 mins

2 cloves garlic, crushed
45ml (3 tablespoons) freshly chopped herbs (parsley, thyme, chives, coriander, marjoram) or 5ml (1 teaspoon) dried herbs

100g (4oz) softened butter
50g (2oz) mature Cheddar cheese, grated
1 large French loaf, cut in half

1. Pre-heat the oven to 400°F (200°C) gas mark 6.
2. Put garlic into a medium-sized mixing bowl. Add herbs and butter. Beat with a wooden spoon to combine, then gradually beat in the cheese to form a soft mixture.
3. Make cuts through each half of the bread at 2.5cm (1in) intervals, but don't cut right through the bottom.
4. Open cuts out and spread with cheese mixture.
5. Smear a little mixture on top of bread, then wrap each half of bread in a piece of foil. Arrange on baking sheet.
6. Bake for 25–30 minutes. Serve immediately. For a crisp top, undo foil and return to oven for last 5 minutes.

Stilton Dip
Serves 6

A light, creamy dip that is ideal with pre-dinner nibbles.

Preparation time: 10 mins
Cooking time: 0

75g (3oz) Stilton cheese   1 × 200ml (7 fl oz) carton
                                       crème fraîche

For the crudités

2 medium carrots   1 red skinned eating apple
1 green skinned eating apple   Lemon juice

1. Put the Stilton into a mixing bowl. Mash with a fork.
2. Gradually beat in the crème fraîche with a wooden spoon.
   Turn into a serving bowl and chill until ready to serve.
3. When ready to serve, cut carrots into matchsticks.
4. Core and slice apples, without peeling. Sprinkle with a little
   lemon juice to prevent discolouration.
5. Serve the bowl of dip in the centre of a large plate, sur-
   rounded by the carrot sticks and apple slices.

Dates with Bacon
Serves 6 (makes 12 tapas)

Often served in Mexican restaurants, these tapas are good served with pre-dinner drinks. Try serving two per person with half a fanned avocado as a starter. Spear each date with a cocktail stick to serve.

Preparation time: 15 mins
Cooking time: 6 mins

6 rashers lean streaky bacon, rinded
12 fresh or dried dates

½ mini le Roule *cheese with herbs and garlic, or approx. 50g (2oz) cream cheese*

1. Stretch the rashers with the back of a knife. Cut each in half vertically.
2. Remove stones from dates. Stuff each date with a little of the cheese.
3. Wrap a half piece of bacon around each date.
4. Arrange on a grill rack and grill for 3–4 minutes on each side. Serve immediately. Alternatively, these tapas may be deep fried in corn oil for a few minutes, then drained on absorbent kitchen paper before serving.

Spiced Cocktail Nuts
Serves 6

These nuts make wonderful pre-dinner nibbles with drinks, so expect them to disappear fast. Serve warm or cold. Once completely cold, store the nuts in an airtight container.

Preparation time: 5 mins
Cooking time: 5 mins

100g (4oz) blanched almonds
100g (4oz) cashew nuts,
* shelled*
100g (4oz) brazil nuts, shelled
* and roughly chopped*

5ml (1 teaspoon) paprika
* pepper*
2.5ml (1/2 teaspoon) medium
* curry powder*
Salt

1. Lay the nuts out in the bottom of a large grill pan.
2. Grill, under a moderate heat, turning the nuts frequently, until lightly toasted.
3. Whilst warm, sprinkle the nuts with paprika pepper, curry powder and salt, tossing to coat.

Salads & Vegetable Dishes

Springtime Pasta Salad
Serves 6

A Continental-style, filling salad that's excellent on the buffet table or served as a quick lunch with chunks of French bread to mop up the juices.

Preparation time: 10 mins
Cooking time: 10 mins

For the salad

225g (8oz) dried pasta twists
225g (8oz) baby carrots, halved or cut into 3
225g (8oz) baby sweetcorn, halved or cut into 3

225g (8oz) mangetout, topped, tailed and halved
100g (4oz) pitted black olives
225g (8oz) smoked mackerel fillet, flaked, discarding skin

For the dressing

85ml (3 fl oz) olive oil
30ml (2 tablespoons) red wine vinegar
5ml (1 teaspoon) clear honey

Salt and freshly ground black pepper
Grated rind of 1 lime

To serve
45ml (3 tablespoons) chopped fresh herbs, such as parsley, thyme and sage

1. In a small bowl, whisk together all the ingredients for the dressing.
2. Cook the pasta in a large pan of boiling water for 5 minutes.

3. Add the carrots, sweetcorn and mangetout to the pan. Return to the boil, then continue to simmer for a further 7 minutes, until 'al dente' (just cooked). Drain well and turn into a large salad bowl. Stir in the olives and the flaked smoked mackerel.

4. Pour dressing over the salad. Toss to coat. Cover and set aside for 10 minutes for the flavours to mingle, then serve.

Chicory Salad
Serves 6

A summery salad that has a super blend of contrasting colour, good texture and taste. The slightly bitter chicory is complemented wonderfully by the sweet oranges.

Preparation time: 10 mins
Cooking time: 0

2 heads chicory
1 Little Gem lettuce

2¹/₂ large oranges, peeled and segmented, membranes removed

For the dressing

2 cloves garlic, crushed
Juice of ¹/₂ orange
45ml (3 tablespoons) olive oil

Salt and freshly ground black pepper
75g (3oz) pecan nuts, chopped

1. Coarsely chop the chicory and put into a salad bowl.
2. Tear the lettuce into bite-sized pieces and add to the bowl with the orange segments.
3. Put the garlic into a small screw-top jar with the orange juice and olive oil. Shake to form an emulsion.
4. Just before serving, pour the dressing over the salad. Toss to coat, sprinkle with pecan nuts and serve.

Dinner Party Mixed Salad
Serves 6

Useful for dinner parties when you need a quick, colourful salad that will accompany meat, fish, poultry or pasta dishes. This quick-to-compile salad with its classic French dressing looks extremely pretty either piled into a wooden salad bowl or arranged on a large white oval dish.

Preparation time: 10 mins
Cooking time: 0

For the salad

100g (4oz) baby spinach leaves
2 Little Gem lettuces, separated into leaves
1 bunch watercress
15ml (1 tablespoon) freshly chopped chives
15ml (1 tablespoon) freshly chopped parsley

1 Mediterranean beef tomato or 2 ripe tomatoes or 50g (2oz) sun-dried tomatoes, drained
2 sticks celery
1/2 yellow pepper, seeded and chopped

For the dressing

90ml (6 tablespoons) virgin olive oil
30ml (2 tablespoons) red wine vinegar

2 cloves garlic, crushed
Salt and freshly ground black pepper

1. Wash and dry the spinach and lettuce in a salad spinner, or dry on a clean tea towel. Tear into bite-sized pieces and put into a salad bowl.
2. Wash watercress, discarding any discoloured leaves. Drain and add to lettuce.
3. Add the chives and parsley. Chop the tomato, discarding the core. Chop the celery roughly and add to the bowl with the yellow pepper.

4. Prepare the dressing by combining the ingredients in a small screw-top jar and shaking briskly.
5. When ready to serve salad, and not before or the dressing will wilt the leaves, sprinkle dressing over salad. Toss lightly to coat, then serve.

Orange, Avocado & Ginger Salad
Serves 6

This salad is pretty in the winter months and useful with duck, beef and oily fish dishes. Serve in a fairly wide, flattish dish.

Preparation time: 10 mins
Cooking time: 0

5 large, seedless oranges
2 ripe avocados
1 × 15g (¹/₂oz) piece Chinese
*   stem ginger in syrup,*
*   drained*

45ml (3 tablespoons) virgin
*   olive oil*
Salt and freshly ground black
*   pepper*
Juice of ¹/₂ lemon

To serve
fresh basil leaves

1. Peel the oranges, holding them over a bowl to catch any drips. Remove all the bitter pith. Slice the oranges thinly and arrange in the serving dish with any juice.
2. Halve the avocados. Remove the stones, then peel the halves and thinly slice the flesh. Add to the serving dish. Chop the ginger fairly finely and add.
3. Put the olive oil into a mug. Add a seasoning of salt and pepper and the lemon juice. Whisk with a fork to combine.
4. Pour dressing over the salad and serve immediately, sprinkled with fresh basil leaves.

Special Green Salad
Serves 6

Pretty frisee lettuce needs careful washing. Lettuce leaves bruise easily when cut with a knife, so it makes sense to tear them into pieces – it's quicker too!

Preparation time: 10 mins
Cooking time: 0

2 Little Gem lettuces
1 small frisee lettuce
1/2 cucumber, cut into
  matchsticks

2 sticks celery, chopped
1 ripe avocado

For the dressing

90ml (6 tablespoons) olive oil
1 clove garlic, crushed
30ml (2 tablespoons) red wine
  vinegar

5ml (1 teaspoon) clear honey
Salt and freshly ground black
  pepper

1. Tear the lettuce leaves into bite-sized pieces and put into a salad bowl with the cucumber and celery.
2. Prepare the dressing. Put all ingredients into a mug and whisk well with a fork.
3. When ready to serve, peel, stone and slice the avocado and add to the bowl.
4. Whisk the dressing again and pour over the salad. Toss to coat.

Greek Salad
Serves 6

This traditional Greek salad makes a wonderful accompaniment to barbecue foods and kebabs. For a speedy lunch, simply fill warmed pitta breads with the salad and serve with some hummus or taramasalata from the deli.

Feta cheese is made from goat's milk. It has a sharp flavour and crumbly texture. Bought in cans or sealed packets, once opened it will keep for 2–3 days in the fridge.

Preparation time: 10 mins
Cooking time: 0

¹/₂ Iceberg lettuce, shredded
¹/₂ cucumber, cubed
1 red pepper, seeded and chopped
1 small red onion, chopped
100g (4oz) pitted black olives
100g (4oz) feta cheese, cubed
60ml (4 tablespoons) olive oil

15ml (1 tablespoon) red wine vinegar
45ml (3 tablespoons) freshly chopped herbs (parsley, sage, mint)
1 clove garlic, crushed
Salt and freshly ground black pepper

1. Put the lettuce into a large bowl. Add the cucumber, red pepper and onion. Toss lightly together.
2. Add the olives and the cheese, then pour on the olive oil and vinegar. Add the herbs, garlic and a light seasoning of salt and pepper.
3. Toss everything together lightly and serve immediately.

Tomato & Bean Salad
with Bacon & Walnut Dressing
Serves 6

A lovely vegetable dish using fresh beans. For a speedier alternative, use 1 × 397g (14oz) can red kidney beans and 1 × 397g (14oz) can sweetcorn instead of the French beans.

Preparation time: 15 mins
Cooking time: 10 mins

450g (1lb) fresh French beans
1 small red skinned onion
225g (8oz) cherry tomatoes, halved
100g (4oz) streaky bacon, rinded
50ml (2 fl oz) walnut oil
15ml (1 tablespoon) red wine vinegar

150ml (5 fl oz) passata
1 clove garlic, crushed
Salt and freshly ground black pepper
1 avocado, peeled and diced
30ml (2 tablespoons) freshly snipped basil

1. Trim the French beans and cook them in a saucepan of boiling water for about 10 minutes, until just tender. Drain and turn into a large bowl.
2. Chop the onion and add to the bowl with the tomatoes.
3. Grill the bacon until crisp, then chop and set aside.
4. In a small bowl, combine the walnut oil with the red wine vinegar, passata and garlic. Season with a little salt and pepper. Whisk with a fork.
5. Pour the dressing over the salad ingredients. Toss to coat. Check seasoning.
6. Stir in the chopped bacon. Top with avocado and basil and serve immediately.

Cracked Wheat Salad with Smoked Trout & Corn
Serves 6

This quick-to-prepare salad is very like rice salad to eat and makes a main meal dish if served with a green salad and bread. Serve 'à tiede' (warm) if you're really pressed for time, or make it earlier in the day and chill in the fridge for 1½ hours for flavours to mingle. Bulghur wheat is available in leading supermarkets. It is commercially made by cracking wheat, then drying and cooking it.

Note: The baguettes are baked, from frozen, in a pre-heated oven 450°F (230°C) gas mark 8 for 8–10 minutes, until crisp and golden. Allow 1 baguette per person.

Preparation time: 10 mins
Cooking time: 8 mins + 30 mins standing time

225g (8oz) bulghur wheat
100g (4oz) frozen sweetcorn kernels
1 × 397g (14oz) can chopped tomatoes
175g (6oz) smoked trout fillet, flaked

30ml (2 tablespoons) freshly chopped parsley
30ml (2 tablespoons) olive oil
30ml (2 tablespoons) soy sauce
10ml (2 teaspoons) Worcestershire sauce
Salt and freshly ground black pepper

To serve
6 frozen, part-baked baguettes (optional)

1. Put the bulghur wheat into a large mixing bowl. Pour over 475ml (16 fl oz) boiling water. Fork through, then cover the bowl with cling film and microwave on 100%/FULL power for 3 minutes.
2. Allow to stand for 30 minutes, covered, then fork up bulghur wheat.
3. Meanwhile, put the sweetcorn into a cereal bowl. Cover and microwave on 100%/FULL power for 5 minutes. Set aside.

4. Once the bulghur wheat has been standing for 30 minutes, it will swell up and look rather like cooked brown rice. Add the sweetcorn, chopped tomatoes, trout, parsley, oil, soy sauce, Worcestershire sauce and a little salt and pepper.

5. Toss well with a fork to mix. Serve immediately or cover and refrigerate until ready to serve. Can be stored overnight in the fridge.

Tomato & Avocado Salad
Serves 6

A colourful salad with a delicious balance of fresh flavours.

Note: If you haven't time to cut all the tomatoes in half, do about three-quarters of them, leaving remainder whole.

Preparation time: 12 mins
Cooking time: 0

225g (8oz) red cherry tomatoes, halved
225g (8oz) yellow cherry tomatoes, halved
1 large avocado
15ml (1 tablespoon) lemon juice
2 spring onions, sliced
30ml (2 tablespoons) raspberry vinegar or red wine vinegar
90ml (6 tablespoons) olive oil
Salt and freshly ground black pepper
2.5ml (1/2 teaspoon) mustard powder
Good pinch caster sugar
15ml (1 tablespoon) freshly snipped chives

1. Put the tomatoes into a large salad bowl.
2. Stone, peel and dice the avocado and sprinkle flesh with lemon juice to prevent discolouring, then add to the tomatoes. Add the spring onions.
3. Prepare the dressing. Put the vinegar and the oil into a mug. Add a little salt and pepper with the mustard and sugar. Whisk with a fork.
4. Pour dressing onto salad. Add chives and toss to combine. Serve immediately.

Tomato & Crab Courgettes Au Gratin
Serves 6

Cheesy courgettes with crab and tomato, toasted quickly under the grill, are perfect for a buffet table. They could also be served as a snack lunch with plenty of crusty bread.

Preparation time: 15 mins
Cooking time: 12 mins

6 medium courgettes, topped and tailed
100g (4oz) Gruyère cheese
1 × 170g (5³/₄oz) can white crab meat or 10 crab sticks, chopped
15ml (1 tablespoon) freshly chopped parsley

15ml (1 tablespoon) olive oil
3 medium tomatoes, peeled and chopped, discarding core
Salt and freshly ground black pepper
15ml (1 tablespoon) grated Italian Pecorino cheese

1. Put the courgettes into a large saucepan. Cover with boiling water. Return to the boil, then simmer, covered, for 5–7 minutes until just tender. Drain.
2. Roughly chop the cooked courgettes and place in a large mixing bowl.
3. Add 75g (3oz) of the Gruyère cheese with the crab meat, parsley, olive oil and tomatoes. Mix well. Season with a little salt and pepper.
4. Turn into a buttered gratin dish. Top with remaining Gruyère cheese. Sprinkle evenly with Pecorino cheese.
5. Pop under a pre-heated grill until cheese is melted and golden. Serve immediately.

Spicy Indian Vegetable Sauté
Serves 6

This spicy vegetable dish goes well with grilled meat, fish and poultry. Cut the carrots and sweetcorn into halves or thirds, depending on size, so they cook in the same time as the beans and mangetout.

Preparation time: 15 mins
Cooking time: 13 mins

1kg (2lb) prepared mixed baby vegetables, such as carrots, beans, sweetcorn, mangetout
45ml (3 tablespoons) olive oil
25g (1oz) butter
5ml (1 teaspoon) ground cumin

5ml (1 teaspoon) ground coriander
15ml (1 tablespoon) fresh root ginger, grated
2 cloves garlic, crushed

To serve
15ml (1 tablespoon) sesame seeds

1. Start by toasting the sesame seeds in a clean heated frying pan. They only take a minute or two, so stir well as they toast for even cooking. Tip onto a plate and set aside.
2. Steam the vegetables for about 8 minutes, until cooked but still firm to the bite.
3. Heat oil and butter in a wok or large frying pan until butter melts.
4. Add cumin and coriander and fry, stirring, for 30 seconds.
5. Add ginger and garlic and stir-fry for a further 30 seconds.
6. Add the steamed vegetables and continue to sauté for about 3 minutes, until just starting to brown.
7. Serve immediately, sprinkled with the toasted sesame seeds.

Chestnut, Celery & Cauliflower Sauté
Serves 6

A well flavoured vegetable dish to serve in the winter months, this is especially useful around Christmas time.

Preparation time: 10 mins
Cooking time: 12 mins

1 × 879g (1lb 15oz) can whole chestnuts, drained
750g (1¹/2lb) cauliflower florets
3 celery stalks
25g (1oz) butter

30ml (2 tablespoons) olive oil
2 medium onions, chopped
Salt and freshly ground black pepper

1. Blot the chestnuts dry with absorbent kitchen paper. Set aside.
2. Cook the cauliflower florets in a large pan of boiling water for 3–4 minutes until just tender. Drain well.
3. Cut the celery into 1.25cm (¹/2in) pieces, on the diagonal.
4. Melt the butter with the olive oil in a wok or large frying pan.
5. Add the celery and onion and sauté for 5 minutes, until softened.
6. Add the chestnuts and the drained cauliflower. Season with a little salt and pepper. Continue to sauté for 2–3 minutes until heated through. Serve immediately.

Speedy Pan Roast Potatoes
Serves 6

Crisp roast potatoes in 35 minutes without par-boiling or waiting for the oven to heat. A firm favourite with almost any main course dish.

Preparation time: 10 mins
Cooking time: 35 mins

*1kg (2lb) white potatoes,
   peeled and cut for roasting
15ml (1 tablespoon) wholemeal
   flour*

*Salt
60ml (4 tablespoons) sunflower
   oil*

1. Blot the peeled potatoes dry with absorbent kitchen paper, then spread out on a dinner plate and sprinkle with the flour (this is easier if you use a flour dredger). Season with a little salt.
2. Heat the oil in a large frying pan, then carefully scoop potatoes into the oil, ensuring they are in a single layer.
3. Cover the pan with a splatter-guard, then cook the potatoes for 30–35 minutes, over a medium heat, turning them individually 3 or 4 times, until crisp and golden on all sides. (They will need the full cooking time to tenderise right through.) Serve immediately.

Cheesy New Potatoes
Serves 6

If you've ever enjoyed 'raclettes' in Switzerland, these tasty potatoes will remind you of them! This dish is delicious on its own, with salad for a speedy lunch or as an accompaniment to beef and fish dishes.

Preparation time: 10 mins
Cooking time: 15 mins

1kg (2lb) new potatoes (Jersey Royals if possible)
1 clove garlic, crushed
50g (2oz) butter
Salt and freshly ground black pepper

100g (4oz) Emmental cheese, grated
30ml (2 tablespoons) grated Parmesan cheese
30ml (2 tablespoons) freshly snipped chives

1. Put the scrubbed potatoes into a large pan and cook in boiling water for about 15 minutes, until tender. Drain and return to pan straightaway so they keep hot.

2. Add the garlic, butter, a little seasoning and the grated Emmental cheese.
3. Return pan to hob used to cook potatoes but don't put it on again (there will be sufficient heat left).
4. Shake the pan gently until butter and cheese just melt.
5. Turn into warmed serving dish and serve immediately, sprinkled with the Parmesan cheese and the chives.

Broccoli with Garlic Crumbs
Serves 6

Broccoli comes in different varieties. Purple sprouting is available in early spring and calabrese (green sprouting) is in the supermarkets from April onwards. Both are delicious. Make the breadcrumbs in the food processor – you will need 3 slices from a large cut loaf, with crusts removed before crumbing.

Preparation time: 15 mins
Cooking time: 12 mins

750g (1½lb) broccoli spears
450ml (15 fl oz) chicken stock
15ml (1 tablespoon) olive oil
15g (½oz) butter
1 large clove garlic, crushed

75g (3oz) fresh brown
 breadcrumbs
Salt and freshly ground black
 pepper

1. In a large saucepan, simmer the broccoli in the chicken stock for 7–8 minutes, until just tender. Drain and keep warm in a covered serving dish.
2. Heat the olive oil with the butter in a medium-sized frying pan until the butter melts.
3. Stir in the garlic and breadcrumbs. Stir-fry for 3–4 minutes until golden. Season well.
4. Spoon over cooked broccoli and serve immediately.

Microwave Magic New Potatoes
Serves 6

Cooked in a trice, microwaved new potatoes have a truly delicious flavour due to the small amount of water needed.

Note: Microwave ovens vary. Test potatoes after standing time. If not quite tender, cover and return to the microwave for a further 2 minutes.

Preparation time: 10 mins
Cooking time: 10 mins + standing time

750g (1¹/₂lb) new potatoes
Sprigs of fresh mint
25g (1oz) butter

15ml (1 tablespoon) freshly
  chopped parsley
Grated rind of 1 lemon

1. Scrub the potatoes clean, then prick each one once with a vegetable knife. Put into a suitable casserole.
2. Add the mint and 45ml (3 tablespoons) water. Cover with a lid and microwave on 100%/FULL power for 10 minutes. Stir and re-cover. Allow to stand for 5 minutes, then drain off the water, add the butter, sprinkle over the parsley and lemon rind, and serve immediately.

Glazed Spring Vegetable Medley
Serves 6

A very easy way to produce vegetables with their own tasty glaze. Vary the recipe using other vegetables in season such as broad beans, cauliflower or courgettes, if you wish.

Preparation time: 10 mins
Cooking time: 12 mins

120ml (4 fl oz) dry white wine
25g (1oz) butter
30ml (2 tablespoons) olive oil
Grated rind of 1/2 lime
Sprig of thyme
450g (1lb) young carrots, halved or cut into three

450g (1lb) small new potatoes
225g (8oz) broccoli florets
Salt and freshly ground black pepper
30ml (2 tablespoons) freshly chopped parsley

1. Put the wine, butter and oil into a large saucepan with the lime rind and thyme. Bring to the boil.
2. Add carrots, potatoes and broccoli florets. Cover and simmer for 12–15 minutes, until tender.
3. Season to taste with a little salt and pepper, then turn contents of pan into a warmed serving dish and serve immediately, sprinkled with the parsley.

Special Rice Pilau
Serves 6

Perfect Basmati rice has an appetisingly aromatic flavour guaranteed to heighten the appetite – a must with all Middle Eastern foods. It is very easy to cook Basmati rice perfectly as long as a few simple rules are followed. Use this foolproof recipe for perfect rice everytime, with very little effort.

Preparation time: 15 mins
Cooking time: 17 mins

350ml (12 fl oz) Basmati white
    rice (measured in a
    measuring jug)
30ml (2 tablespoons) sunflower
    oil
1 small onion, chopped
1 clove garlic, crushed
2.5ml (½ teaspoon) powdered
    saffron

1 bay leaf
5ml (1 teaspoon) cumin seeds,
    crushed
Salt and freshly ground black
    pepper
75g (3oz) raisins
75g (3oz) shelled pistachio
    nuts, roughly chopped

1. Put the rice into a sieve and wash under cold running water for 2–3 minutes, turning rice with your hand, until well rinsed and water is no longer running cloudy.
2. Transfer rice to a bowl, cover with cold water and set aside for 5 minutes.
3. Heat the oil in a large saucepan. Add onion and garlic and sauté for 5 minutes, until onion softens.
4. Drain rice through a sieve, then add to the pan with the saffron, bay leaf and cumin seeds.
5. Sauté rice for 1–2 minutes until glossy.
6. Add a seasoning of salt and pepper and 720ml (24 fl oz) water.
7. Bring to the boil, stirring once. Cover and simmer gently until liquid is absorbed and rice is tender (about 10 minutes). Do not stir during this time.
8. Remove the bay leaf and stir in the raisins. Fluff up and serve immediately, sprinkled with the pistachio nuts.

Risotto with Kidney Beans, Apricots and Cashew Nuts
Serves 6

A specially tasty risotto that will appeal to all. Serve with a tomato salad.

Preparation time: 15 mins
Cooking time: 33 mins

60ml (4 tablespoons) olive oil
1 onion, chopped
350g (12oz) easy-cook brown rice
3 cloves garlic, crushed
900ml (1¹/₂ pints) light vegetable stock
100g (4oz) cashew nuts

3 celery stalks, chopped
100g (4oz) mangetout, halved
225g (8oz) mushrooms, sliced
1 × 425g (15oz) can red kidney beans, drained
50g (2oz) dried apricots, chopped

To garnish
30ml (2 tablespoons) freshly chopped parsley or *grated Parmesan cheese*

1. Heat 30ml (2 tablespoons) of the oil in a large saucepan. Sauté the onion for 3–4 minutes, until softened. Add the rice and stir briefly to coat with oil.
2. Add the garlic and the stock. Bring to the boil, then cover and simmer for 25 minutes until all the water has been absorbed and the rice is tender.
3. Meanwhile, heat remaining oil in a large frying pan or wok, add the nuts, celery, mangetout and mushrooms. Stir-fry for 3–4 minutes.
4. Add the red kidney beans, dried apricots and rice to the frying pan or wok. Continue to cook, stirring until thoroughly hot.
5. Serve immediately, sprinkled with parsley or Parmesan cheese.

Flashy Jackets
Serves 6

This is a very simple way to jazz up baked potatoes. Using the microwave cuts the cooking time by half.

Preparation time: 5 mins
Cooking time: 36 mins

*6 old white potatoes, each
    weighing approx 175g (6oz)*

Olive oil, for brushing
Salt

To serve
150ml (5 fl oz) soured cream

*15ml (1 tablespoon) freshly
    chopped chives*

1. Wash the potatoes and blot dry with absorbent kitchen paper. Make a cross in the top of each one with a sharp knife and arrange in a circle on a dinner plate. Brush with olive oil. Sprinkle with salt.

2. Pre-heat the oven to 400°F (200°C) gas mark 6.
3. Put the potatoes into the microwave and microwave on 100%/FULL power for 16 minutes.
4. Transfer potatoes to a lightly oiled roasting tin and bake in the pre-heated oven for 20 minutes, until tender.
5. Serve the potatoes with the soured cream and chives. (If you push the potatoes up from the base using a clean cloth, they will form water lily shapes.)

Tomato & Courgette Gratin
Serves 6

An ideal vegetarian dish. Excellent, too, as an accompaniment to roast meats, chicken and grilled foods. Try this dish in late summer when courgettes and tomatoes are plentiful and cheap. The quickest way to make the topping is to put the cheese and bread, torn into pieces, into the food processor and process until finely chopped.

Preparation time: 12 mins
Cooking time: 35 mins

60ml (4 tablespoons) olive oil
2 large onions, chopped
2 cloves garlic, crushed
750g (1¹/₂lb) courgettes, sliced
1 small green pepper, seeded and chopped

1 × 400g (14oz) can chopped tomatoes
30ml (2 tablespoons) freshly chopped herbs (parsley, thyme, oregano, marjoram)
Salt and freshly ground black pepper

For the topping

25g (1oz) Gruyère cheese, grated or cubed if using a food processor

50g (2oz) wholemeal bread

1. Pre-heat the oven to 375°F (190°C) gas mark 5.
2. Lightly oil a 1.75 litre (3 pint) oval gratin dish.
3. Heat 30ml (2 tablespoons) of the oil in a large frying pan. Sauté the onions and garlic for 5 minutes, until softened. Remove with a draining spoon and put into base of oiled dish.
4. Add remaining oil to the pan and heat. Add courgettes and green pepper. Sauté for 10 minutes. Add contents of pan and the tomatoes to the gratin dish.
5. Sprinkle over the herbs and season with salt and pepper. Sprinkle over the cheese and breadcrumbs.

6. Bake for 25 minutes until crisp and lightly golden. Serve immediately.
   Note: If the topping doesn't seem to brown sufficiently in the oven, pop it under a hot grill for a couple of minutes before serving.

Herby Vegetable Purée
Serves 6

Try tempting anyone who thinks they don't really like swede with this tasty combination. Delicious for dinner parties and wonderful with the turkey on Christmas Day. The purée re-heats well in the microwave if you wish to prepare it in advance.

To re-heat the purée in the microwave, cover the vegetable dish with cling film and microwave on 100%/FULL power for 3–4 minutes. Stir the purée then serve, sprinkled with the herbs.

Note: For a speedier vegetable dish, serve the drained, cooked vegetables, sprinkled with the fresh herbs as a pretty vegetable medley.

Preparation time: 10 mins
Cooking time: 35 mins

1kg (2lb) swede, peeled and diced into 1.25cm (1/2in) dice
3 celery stalks, chopped finely
225g (8oz) young carrots, diced
10ml (2 teaspoons) dried parsley
2 cloves garlic, crushed

150ml (5 fl oz) vegetable stock
25g (1oz) butter
60ml (4 tablespoons) medium sweet cider or white or red wine
Freshly ground black pepper
30ml (2 tablespoons) double cream

To serve
freshly chopped parsley   *snipped chives*

1. Put the vegetables into a large, flameproof casserole with a lid.
2. Add the dried parsley, garlic, stock, butter and cider or wine.
3. Season with about eight grinds of pepper.
4. Cover with a tightly fitting lid and simmer for about 30 minutes, stirring once or twice, until vegetables are quite tender.

5. Remove from heat. Turn contents of pan into food processor and blend to a purée.
6. Stir in cream. Return to pan and re-heat gently, stirring, but do not allow to boil. Turn into a large vegetable dish and serve sprinkled with fresh parsley and chives.

Fruity Relish
Serves 6

Relishes are crisp, moist and refreshing – the ideal accompaniments to barbecue foods, roasts and fish dishes. Simple and quick to put together, they immediately add flavour and colour to whatever you choose to serve them with.

Note: Don't worry too much if you can't get red onions; the recipe works well with brown skinned onions.

Preparation time: 10 mins
Cooking time: 0

2 medium red onions, coarsely chopped
100g (4oz) ready-to-use dried apricots
1 × 142ml (4¹/2 fl oz) carton soured cream

Salt and freshly ground black pepper
Grated rind and juice of ¹/2 orange

1. Put the onions into a large bowl and cover with boiling water. Allow to stand for 3 minutes, then drain and return to bowl. Set aside.
2. Snip the apricots into small pieces, using scissors, and add to the onions with the soured cream and a seasoning of salt and pepper.
3. Fold in the grated orange rind and juice and serve immediately.

Courgette & Corn Relish
Serves 6

A wonderful combination of natural flavours that's colourful and appealing. Hand the relish round in a bowl. Everyone loves this fresh, crunchy salad addition.

Preparation time: 10 mins
Cooking time: 5 mins

175g (6oz) frozen sweetcorn kernels
4 baby courgettes, ends discarded
1/2 red pepper, seeded and finely diced
1/2 onion or 3 spring onions, finely chopped
30ml (2 tablespoons) chopped chives
1 × 400g (14oz) can chopped tomatoes
1 clove garlic, crushed (optional)
30ml (2 tablespoons) olive oil
Salt and freshly ground black pepper

1. If you have a microwave, put the sweetcorn into a casserole dish with 15ml (1 tablespoon) water. Cover with a lid and microwave on 100%/FULL power for 5 minutes. Alternatively, cook the sweetcorn conventionally in a little boiling water in a covered pan, according to directions on the packet.
2. Turn the drained sweetcorn into a large mixing bowl.
3. Cut the courgettes into fairly small dice and add to the bowl with the red pepper.
4. Add to the bowl the onion with the chives, chopped tomatoes, garlic and olive oil. Season with a little salt and pepper.
5. Toss well to mix, then serve immediately.

Main Courses

Oven-fried Indian Chicken
Serves 6

Chicken cooked in a spicy glaze is tasty and popular. Serve with an orange salad and a bowl of Little Gem lettuce leaves tossed in a minty vinaigrette. French bread or boiled rice would complete the meal. If you can leave the chicken in the glaze for a little longer before cooking, so much the better. Prepare earlier in the day or even the night before. Simply cover the dish and chill in the fridge until ready to cook.

Note: To toast the nuts, arrange on a baking sheet and bake in the oven for 5–10 minutes, until golden.

Preparation time: 10 mins
Cooking time: 40 mins

6 fresh chicken quarters
15ml (1 tablespoon) grated fresh root ginger
10ml (2 teaspoons) medium hot curry powder
5ml (1 teaspoon) paprika pepper

15ml (1 tablespoon) freshly snipped basil
2.5ml (1/2 teaspoon) ground nutmeg
15ml (1 tablespoon) clear honey
45ml (3 tablespoons) olive oil
Salt

To serve
100g (4oz) toasted cashew nuts (optional)

1. Trim the chicken quarters, leaving the skin on. Arrange them, skin side up, in a large roasting tin.
2. Pre-heat the oven to 425°F (220°C) gas mark 7.
3. Put the ginger into a small mixing bowl. Add the curry powder, paprika, basil, nutmeg, honey and olive oil. Season with a little salt and mix well.
4. Spoon the honey glaze evenly over the chicken. Set aside for 10 minutes.

5. Cover the dish with foil and put into oven, near the top, for 20 minutes.
6. Remove foil and discard. Baste chicken with juices then return to oven for a further 20 minutes, until golden. (Baste again after 10 minutes to encourage chicken to brown.)
7. Pierce with a sharp knife to ensure chicken is cooked – juices must run clear. Serve immediately, sprinkled with the cashew nuts, if using.

Stir-fry Spicy Chicken with Cashew Nuts
Serves 6

This should be served as part of a multi-dish Chinese meal.

Preparation time: 10 mins
Cooking time: 12 mins

30ml (2 tablespoons) sunflower oil
50g (2oz) cashew nuts
15ml (1 tablespoon) grated fresh root ginger
6 spring onions, chopped
1 stick celery, finely chopped
¼ teaspoon dried chillies
750g (1½lb) chicken breast fillet, skinned and thinly sliced

16 fresh baby corn, halved lengthways
225g (8oz) mangetout, topped, tailed and halved
100g (4oz) button mushrooms, sliced
150ml (5 fl oz) orange juice
15ml (1 tablespoon) soy sauce
5ml (1 teaspoon) cornflour

1. Heat the oil in a wok. Add the cashew nuts and stir-fry until golden. Remove using a draining spoon and blot on absorbent kitchen paper.
2. Add the ginger, spring onions, celery, chillies and chicken to the pan. Stir-fry for 3–4 minutes until chicken is browned all over.
3. Add the corn, mangetout and mushrooms and stir-fry for 4–5 minutes, until just tender.
4. Blend together the orange juice, soy sauce and cornflour, and stir into the pan. Bring to the boil, stirring. Simmer for 2 minutes.
5. Serve immediately, topped with the cashew nuts.

Apricot Chicken

Serves 6

This fresh fruity recipe makes a delicious dinner party or quick, special lunch dish. Serve with new potatoes and the Dinner Party Mixed Salad on page 50.

Preparation time: 5 mins
Cooking time: 25 mins

45ml (3 tablespoons) sunflower oil
6 boneless chicken breasts, skinned
15ml (1 tablespoon) arrowroot
1 × 425g (15oz) can apricot halves, in natural juice, drained, reserving juice

150ml (5 fl oz) chicken stock
45ml (3 tablespoons) dry cider
5ml (1 teaspoon) soft brown sugar
5ml (1 teaspoon) ground coriander
30ml (2 tablespoons) freshly chopped parsley

To garnish
2 oranges, sliced

1. Heat the oil in a large frying pan. Fry the chicken breasts on all sides, until golden.
2. In a mixing jug, blend the arrowroot with the apricot juice.

Add to the pan with the chicken stock and the cider. Bring to the boil, stirring.

3. Add the sugar, coriander, 15ml (1 tablespoon) of the parsley and the apricot halves. Stir gently.

4. Cover the pan and simmer for 15–20 minutes, until chicken is cooked.

5. To serve, lift the chicken and apricots onto a warmed serving dish. Pour sauce over. Sprinkle with remaining parsley and garnish with the sliced oranges.

Chicken & Walnuts in Red Wine
Serves 6

This colourful dish presents succulent chicken breasts and pretty vegetables cooked together in one pan with a sauce. Serve with pan-fried roast potatoes sprinkled with plenty of chopped fresh parsley. The frozen boneless chicken breasts, now available from most leading supermarkets, would be ideal for this recipe.

Preparation time: 10 mins
Cooking time: 35 mins

15ml (1 tablespoon) olive oil
25g (1oz) butter
6 boneless, skinned chicken breasts, defrosted if frozen
225g (8oz) carrots, sliced on diagonal
1/2 medium onion, chopped

350g (12oz) baby courgettes, sliced on diagonal
300ml (10 fl oz) light chicken or vegetable stock
150ml (5 fl oz) red wine
Freshly ground black pepper
22.5ml (1 1/2 tablespoons) cornflour

To serve
50g (2oz) chopped walnuts   *freshly chopped parsley*

1. Heat oil and butter in a large frying pan.
2. Add chicken breasts, in a single layer. Fry over a fairly high heat, turning until sealed and golden on all sides. Transfer to a dinner plate.
3. Add carrots, onion and courgettes to pan and sauté for 5 minutes.
4. Lay chicken pieces back in pan, on the bed of vegetables.
5. Add stock and wine and season with a little black pepper.
6. Bring to the boil, then cover and simmer for 25 minutes, until chicken is tender. Lift chicken breasts onto serving dish.
7. Toast walnuts briefly under pre-heated grill. Set aside.

8. Mix cornflour to a smooth paste with a little water. Stir into pan. Continue to simmer for 1–2 minutes, stirring continuously.

9. Serve the chicken with a little of the sauce poured over, sprinkled with the walnuts and the freshly chopped parsley. Serve remaining sauce separately.

Quick Chicken Curry
Serves 6

This lightly flavoured curry uses cooked chicken, but you could use cooked turkey, pork or lamb if preferred.

Preparation time: 15 mins
Cooking time: 37 mins

30ml (2 tablespoons) sunflower oil
2 large onions, sliced
1 clove garlic, crushed
2 sticks celery, chopped
2 carrots, diced
15ml (1 tablespoon) plain flour
15ml (1 tablespoon) medium Madras curry powder
10ml (2 teaspoons) curry paste
Salt
2.5ml (1/2 teaspoon) turmeric

2.5ml (1/2 teaspoon) coriander
2.5ml (1/2 teaspoon) oregano
600ml (1 pint) chicken stock
15ml (1 tablespoon) lemon juice
750g (1 1/2lb) cooked chicken, roughly chopped
45ml (3 tablespoons) fromage frais
50g (2oz) toasted flaked almonds

To serve
boiled rice

1. Heat oil in a large saucepan. Add onion, garlic, celery and carrot. Sauté for 5–7 minutes, until softened.
2. Add flour and curry powder, curry paste and a light seasoning of salt.
3. Stir in the turmeric, coriander and oregano.
4. Gradually stir in the chicken stock and the lemon juice. Bring to the boil.
5. Cover and simmer for 20 minutes, then stir in the chicken. Simmer for 10 minutes, then stir in the fromage frais and re-heat gently, without boiling.
6. Serve the chicken curry topped with the almonds and accompanied by a pan of boiled rice.

Sesame Seed Chicken
Serves 6

These part-boned chicken breasts can be cooked on the barbecue or under a pre-heated grill. Serve with mangetout and the salsa on page 128. Warm granary bread rolls would complete the meal.

Preparation time: 10 mins
Cooking time: 30 mins

2 cloves garlic, crushed
45ml (3 tablespoons) olive oil
6 part-boned chicken breasts, each weighing approx. 225g (8oz)
Salt and freshly ground black pepper

30ml (2 tablespoons) freshly chopped coriander
30ml (2 tablespoons) clear honey
15ml (1 tablespoon) sesame seeds

To garnish
wedges of orange   *sprigs of coriander*

1. Pre-heat the grill to medium hot. Lightly oil the grill pan.
2. Place the crushed garlic and the olive oil in a small bowl.
3. Slash each chicken breast in three places with a sharp knife. This helps them to cook more quickly and prevents them drying out.
4. Brush chicken all over with the garlicky oil. Season with a little salt and pepper and sprinkle with the coriander.
5. Cook the chicken under the pre-heated grill for approx. 30 minutes, turning two or three times. They are cooked when juices run clear if pierced with a sharp knife.
6. Brush chicken skin all over with the honey and sprinkle with sesame seeds. Continue to grill until crisp and golden.
7. Transfer to a warmed serving dish and keep warm for 10 minutes. Serve garnished with the orange wedges and coriander.

Barbecue Drumsticks
Serves 6

Chicken with a kick that's cooked in an instant. Great for a speedy lunch, also good for 'al fresco' eating, picnics and buffets. Cook on the barbecue, if preferred. Line the grill rack with foil, then lightly oil the foil before cooking the chicken. Serve with mixed salad and pitta bread, warmed in the oven for a few minutes.

Preparation time: 10 mins
Cooking time: 15–20 mins

12 chicken drumsticks, fresh if possible
30ml (2 tablespoons) tomato purée
15ml (1 tablespoon) clear honey
Juice of ½ lemon
1 clove garlic, crushed
15ml (1 tablespoon) soy sauce
Freshly ground black pepper
10ml (2 teaspoons) sesame seeds

1. Skin the chicken – it's easiest to grip the skin with absorbent kitchen paper and tear it off fairly quickly in one piece.
2. Put the chicken into a shallow container and pre-heat the grill to moderately hot.
3. In a small bowl mix together the tomato purée, honey, lemon juice, garlic and soy sauce. Season with a little pepper.
4. Brush the barbecue glaze evenly all over the drumsticks. Arrange on grill rack. Sprinkle with sesame seeds.
5. Cook for 15–20 minutes, turning two or three times, until browned and juices run clear when chicken is pierced with a sharp knife. Serve warm or cold.

Mini Chicken Tikkas
Serves 6

For a more pronounced flavour, the chicken could be prepared earlier in the day, or even overnight and kept in the fridge, covered, until ready to grill. You will need six wooden skewers, soaked in water for at least 20 minutes before use to prevent them burning under the grill.

Note: For chicken satay, use the satay marinade on page 209 instead of the yoghurt mixture described here.

Preparation time: 15 mins
Cooking time: 15 mins

750g (1¹/₂lb) chicken breast
  fillet, skinned
150ml (5 fl oz) natural yoghurt
15ml (1 tablespoon) lemon
  juice

10ml (2 teaspoons) paprika
2.5ml (¹/₂ teaspoon) hot chilli
  powder
1 clove garlic, crushed
Salt

To serve
cucumber slices   raw onion slices

1. Dice chicken into 2.5cm (1in) cubes.
2. Put yoghurt, lemon juice, paprika, chilli powder and garlic into a mixing bowl. Stir to blend. Season with a little salt. Add chicken and stir to coat.
3. Set aside for 15 minutes for flavours to penetrate chicken.
4. Thread the chicken onto the skewers and grill or barbecue for 10–15 minutes, until golden brown and tender. Turn the chicken occasionally during cooking.
5. Serve the chicken immediately with the cucumber and onion.

Oriental Turkey Stir-fry
Serves 6

Stir-fry is a quick method of cooking the main part of the meal in one large pan over a high heat. Ensure everything is ready before you start to cook.

Preparation time: 12 mins
Cooking time: 13 mins

5ml (1 teaspoon) dried parsley
2 Chinese stock cubes, crumbled
10ml (2 teaspoons) cornflour
30ml (2 tablespoons) dry white wine
5ml (1 teaspoon) soy sauce
30ml (2 tablespoons) olive oil
750g (1¹/₂lb) boneless turkey breast, cut into thin strips

1 large onion, chopped
2 carrots, thinly sliced, then slices halved into half-moons
2 sticks celery, finely chopped
1 red pepper, seeded and chopped
100g (4oz) button mushrooms, sliced

To serve
fresh sprigs of basil   *boiled noodles*

1. In a measuring jug, combine the dried parsley, Chinese stock cubes, cornflour, white wine and soy sauce with 300ml (10 fl oz) water. Stir to blend cornflour.
2. Heat the olive oil in a wok. Stir-fry the turkey for 4–5 minutes, over a high heat, until browned all over.
3. Add prepared onion, carrots, celery, red pepper and mushrooms to the pan and continue to stir-fry for a further 4–5 minutes, until vegetables soften slightly.
4. Add contents of measuring jug to the wok. Bring to the boil, stirring. Simmer for 1–2 minutes, until slightly thickened, then serve garnished with the basil, on a bed of noodles.

Duck with Blackcurrant Sauce
Serves 6

Barbary ducks from France are best for this recipe, but if you can't get them, English ones will do. Accompany the duck with fresh asparagus or mangetout and new potatoes, glazed with butter or olive oil, tossed in plenty of freshly chopped parsley.

Preparation time: 15 mins
Cooking time: 30 mins

6 boneless duck breasts, with skin, each weighing 175–225g (6–8oz)

Salt and freshly ground black pepper
15ml (1 tablespoon) dried basil

For the sauce

350g (12oz) blackcurrants, removed from stems
50g (2oz) caster sugar

450ml (15 fl oz) chicken stock
15ml (1 tablespoon) arrowroot
45ml (3 tablespoons) port

To garnish
sprigs of coriander

1. Pre-heat the oven to 400°F (200°C) gas mark 6.
2. Slash the skins on each duck breast two or three times (this speeds up cooking and prevents them drying out).
3. Place on rack in a roasting tin. Season with salt and pepper, then sprinkle with basil.
4. Bake for 20–30 minutes, depending on how well done you like duck.
5. Meanwhile, make the sauce. Put blackcurrants, sugar, stock and arrowroot into a medium-sized saucepan. Stir well.
6. Bring to the boil, stirring, then simmer for 5 minutes, stirring occasionally.
7. Sieve sauce and return to pan, stir in the port. Re-heat gently.
8. To serve, cut breasts into fans, diagonally across the grain, and arrange on a warmed serving dish. Garnish with coriander and serve with a pool of the re-heated sauce, offering remaining sauce in a sauce boat.

Fanned Duckling with Whisky Sauce & Kumquats

Serves 4

Duck with whisky and kumquats is deliciously different and makes a pretty dinner party main course. Kumquats should be seedless, but unfortunately they do now sometimes have pips.

Preparation time: 10 mins
Cooking time: 13 mins

25g (1oz) butter
10ml (2 teaspoons) olive oil
4 boneless duckling breasts
25ml (1 tablespoon + 2
   teaspoons) cornflour
Grated rind of 1 orange
Juice of 2 oranges
5ml (1 teaspoon) lemon juice
Salt and freshly ground black
   pepper

300ml (10 fl oz) chicken stock
30ml (2 tablespoons) coarse
   cut orange marmalade
45ml (3 tablespoons) whisky
8 kumquats, sliced and seeded
15ml (1 tablespoon) fresh
   root ginger, cut into fine
   strips

To serve
wedges of lime   sprigs of fresh mint

1. Heat the butter and olive oil in a frying pan until butter melts. Add the duckling breasts, skin side down, and cook for about 6 minutes until lightly browned.
2. Turn breasts over and continue to cook for about 5 minutes, or until cooked through.
3. Remove duck from pan, cover and keep warm.
4. Blend cornflour with the orange rind and juice, the lemon juice and a little seasoning. Add to the pan with stock and marmalade. Heat gently, stirring, until marmalade dissolves.
5. Gradually bring to the boil, stirring. Add the whisky, kumquats and ginger, and simmer for 1–2 minutes.

6. Cut the duck breasts into thin slices, leaving the skin on or removing, as preferred.
7. Arrange the duck on four warmed dinner plates, in a fan shape overlapping the slices at one end.
8. Pour the sauce over the duck. Decorate with the lime and mint, and serve immediately.

Spicy Lamb & Tomatoes
Serves 6

Serve this Middle Eastern style dish with jacket potatoes or rice and the yoghurt sauce on page 88. Ideal for lunch or dinner parties.

If time allows, remove any bitter juices from the aubergine using the method described on page 11.

Preparation time: 10 mins
Cooking time: 28 mins

45ml (3 tablespoons) olive oil
1 medium onion, chopped
2 cloves garlic, crushed
1 aubergine, about 350g (12oz), diced
1kg (2lb) raw, lean minced lamb
1 × 400g (14oz) can tomatoes in tomato juice
225g (8oz) chopped frozen leaf spinach

2.5ml (¹/2 teaspoon) dried chopped chillies
5ml (1 teaspoon) ground turmeric
5ml (1 teaspoon) dried oregano
85ml (3 fl oz) red wine
Salt and freshly ground black pepper
10ml (2 teaspoons) garam masala

To serve
freshly chopped mint

1. Heat the oil in a large flameproof casserole dish or saucepan.
2. Add the onion, garlic and aubergine to the pan and sauté for 3–4 minutes, until vegetables soften and start to brown. Remove using a draining spoon and set aside.
3. Add the lamb to the pan and sauté for 3–4 minutes, until just starting to brown. Return onion, garlic and aubergine to the pan.
4. Add all remaining ingredients, except garam masala and mint. Stir well, seasoning with a little salt and pepper.
5. Bring to simmering point, stirring, then cover and simmer for 20 minutes. Stir in the garam masala.
6. Serve immediately, sprinkled with the fresh mint.

Shish Kebabs

Serves 6 (makes approx. 30 kebabs)

Tempting, mint-flavoured lamb, grilled until brown and succulent. Serve with plain yoghurt topped with a shake of paprika. A crisp mixed salad and warm pitta bread would go well with the shish kebabs. If preferred, serve the meat balls on a plate of freshly cooked rice.

Preparation time: 15 mins
Cooking time: 20 mins

750g (1¹/₂lb) raw minced lamb
1 large onion, finely chopped
Juice of ¹/₂ lemon
15ml (1 tablespoon) medium Madras curry powder
15ml (1 tablespoon) fromage frais

1 egg, size 4, beaten
40g (1¹/₂oz) plain flour
30ml (2 tablespoons) freshly chopped mint
2.5ml (¹/₂ teaspoon) salt
10ml (2 teaspoons) tomato purée

To serve
chopped parsley

1. Pre-heat the grill and lightly oil the upside-down grill rack.
2. Make the shish kebabs. Put the lamb into a large mixing bowl. Add all remaining ingredients. Mix well, then roll into small balls or ovals – it will help if you do this with wet hands.
3. Grill the shish kebabs in two batches, for approx. 5 minutes each side, until browned. Transfer each batch to a serving dish and keep warm whilst you cook the remainder.
4. Serve immediately, sprinkled with the freshly chopped parsley.

Glazed Pork with Marmalade Sauce
Serves 6

Pork with a tangy orange-flavoured sauce makes a refreshing change from duck. Serve with jacket potatoes and courgettes.

Preparation time: 15 mins
Cooking time: 15 mins

175g (6oz) thick cut orange marmalade
1 clove garlic, crushed
15ml (1 tablespoon) olive oil
10ml (2 teaspoons) cornflour
3 spring onions, roughly chopped
150ml (5 fl oz) vegetable stock
150ml (5 fl oz) dry white wine

15ml (1 tablespoon) soy sauce
5ml (1 teaspoon) grated fresh root ginger
15ml (1 tablespoon) freshly chopped parsley
Salt and freshly ground black pepper
6 pork chop fillets

To garnish
sprigs of watercress

1. Put marmalade, garlic, oil, cornflour, spring onions, stock, white wine, soy sauce, ginger and parsley into a medium-sized saucepan. Season with a little salt and pepper. Cook over a medium heat, stirring continuously, until a smooth sauce results (about 5 minutes).
2. Put the chops into a shallow dish in a single layer.
3. Pour over about 60ml (4 tablespoons) of the sauce, then set the chops aside for 10 minutes. Return sauce to heat and simmer gently until ready to serve chops.
4. Pre-heat grill to medium hot. Lightly oil the rack.
5. Lift chops onto grill rack, returning any sauce left in dish to the saucepan. Grill pork for 10–15 minutes until cooked through, turning chops once or twice.
6. To serve, transfer chops to warmed serving dish. Spoon over a little of the sauce. Garnish with watercress and serve, handing remaining sauce round in a jug.

Chinese Spare Ribs
Serves 6

If possible, prepare the Chinese ribs in the morning, then all you have to do is roast them on a rack for 30 minutes before serving with barbecue sauce, salad and French bread, or split jacket potatoes filled with sour cream and chives.

Note: If you prefer, instead of oven roasting, these spare rib chops may be grilled or cooked on the barbecue.

Preparation time: 10 mins **+** marinating time
Cooking time: 20–30 mins

18 skinned belly of pork ribs

For the marinade

60ml (4 tablespoons) clear honey
60ml (4 tablespoons) soy sauce
1 clove garlic, crushed
2.5cm (1in) piece fresh ginger, peeled and grated
Grated rind and juice 1 orange
30ml (2 tablespoons) tomato purée
5ml (1 teaspoon) dried parsley
Salt and freshly ground black pepper

1. In a mixing bowl, combine all ingredients for the marinade. Mix well.
2. Arrange pork ribs in a large, shallow dish. Brush marinade over with pastry brush.
3. Set aside, covered, for 20 minutes, or refrigerate overnight. Turn in marinade once, if you're around.
4. Pre-heat the oven to 475°F (240°C) gas mark 9.
5. Arrange ribs on rack in roasting pan (or directly onto roasting pan if you don't possess a rack).
6. Roast for 20–30 minutes, until dark brown, basting with the juices after 10 and 15 minutes.
7. Serve immediately with the barbecue sauce on page 127.

Spicy Sausage & Wine Casserole
Serves 6

A wonderful casserole to serve on Bonfire Night or on any cold winter's evening, this is popular with young people as well as adults. Serve with jacket potatoes and salad, or plenty of fresh bread. Buy Kabanos (Continental sausage) from the deli counter.

Preparation time: 15 mins
Cooking time: 35 mins

30ml (2 tablespoons) sunflower oil
450g (1lb) best quality pork sausages
225g (8oz) herby pork sausages
1 large onion, chopped
1 red pepper, seeded and chopped
1 green pepper, seeded and chopped
225g (8oz) Kabanos

15ml (1 tablespoon) mild paprika pepper
1 × 400g (14oz) can chopped tomatoes with herbs
45ml (3 tablespoons) tomato purée
150ml (5 fl oz) red wine
1 stock cube
Salt and freshly ground black pepper
1 × 430g (15oz) can red kidney beans, drained

To garnish
freshly chopped basil or parsley

1. In a large saucepan or casserole heat the oil.
2. Brown the uncooked sausages all over. (You may have to do this in two batches.) Remove using a slotted spoon. (The Kabanos do not need browning.)
3. Fry onions and peppers in remaining oil for 3 minutes.
4. Cut all sausages into 2.5cm (1in) pieces and return to pan.
5. Add paprika, tomatoes, tomato purée and red wine to the pan.
6. Crumble in the stock cube. Season with a little salt and pepper. Stir well, cover and simmer for 25 minutes.
7. Add beans and heat through thoroughly, stirring.
8. Check seasoning, then serve sprinkled with the basil or parsley.

Smoked Ham & Emmental Salad
Serves 6

A light main meal salad dish that's suitable for summer lunches or winter buffet menus. Warmed French stick is delicious with this recipe.

Preparation time: 10 mins
Cooking time: 0

175g (6oz) smoked ham, diced
3 sticks celery, chopped
175g (6oz) Emmental cheese, cubed
2 red eating apples
10ml (2 teaspoons) white wine vinegar

150ml (5 fl oz) soured cream
15ml (1 tablespoon) freshly chopped coriander
Salt and freshly ground black pepper
25g (1oz) chopped walnuts
Paprika pepper

To serve
mixed lettuce leaves

1. Put the ham into a large mixing bowl with the celery and the cheese.
2. Core and chop the apples and add to the bowl.
3. Add the white wine vinegar, soured cream, coriander and a seasoning of salt and pepper.
4. Toss well. Chill, covered, for 5–10 minutes.
5. To serve, arrange salad leaves on base of an oval plate. Pile ham mixture into centre. Sprinkle with walnuts and paprika and serve immediately.

Ham & Apricot Terrine
Serves 6

Good for 'al fresco' eating and excellent on the buffet table too. Serve this tasty savoury, well chilled, in slices. You will need a 1kg (2lb) loaf tin.

Preparation time: 15 mins
Cooking time: 5 mins

750g (1½lb) cooked ham (a mixture of smoked and unsmoked is nice)
45ml (3 tablespoons) freshly chopped parsley
30ml (2 tablespoons) freshly chopped tarragon
2 cloves garlic, crushed

100g (4oz) dried apricots, chopped
Salt and freshly ground black pepper
1 × 24g (1oz) packet aspic jelly powder
90ml (6 tablespoons) medium sweet cider (see method)

To serve
salad leaf garnish

1. Cut ham into thin shreds and put into a mixing bowl.
2. Add chopped herbs, garlic and apricots. Season lightly with salt and pepper. Toss together to mix, then turn into the loaf tin.
3. Make up aspic according to packet instructions, substituting the cider for 90ml (6 tablespoons) of the water. Pour over ham mixture. Chill in refrigerator for 4 hours, until set, or overnight.
4. To serve, dip terrine in hot water and hold for 10 seconds. Invert onto serving plate. Shake to release terrine. Garnish terrine with salad leaves and serve immediately.

Steak à l'orange
Serves 6

Pan-fried fillet steak with a fresh tasting fruity sauce. Wonderful
with new potatoes and broccoli.

Preparation time: 10 mins
Cooking time: 6 mins

*6 fillet steaks, about 2cm (³/₄in)
  thick*

*Salt and freshly ground black
  pepper
50g (2oz) butter*

For the sauce

*150ml (5 fl oz) medium cider
Rind of 1 orange
Juice of 2 oranges, strained
Juice of 1 lemon, strained
15ml (1 tablespoon) clear
  honey*

*5ml (1 teaspoon) red wine
  vinegar
15ml (1 tablespoon) cornflour
5ml (1 teaspoon) dried
  tarragon*

To garnish
sprigs of watercress

1. Season the steaks on both sides with a little salt and pepper.
2. Melt the butter in a large frying pan. When foaming, add the
   steaks. Seal on both sides over a high heat, then lower the
   heat to medium and cook the steaks for approx 2½ minutes
   for rare, 3½ minutes for medium or 4 minutes for well done.
   Remove steaks from pan, put on a warmed serving dish and
   keep warm.
3. Put all ingredients for the sauce into a jug. Stir to blend
   cornflour.
4. Pour sauce ingredients into frying pan. Bring to boil, stirring.
   Simmer for 1–2 minutes, stirring. Season to taste.
5. Serve the steaks with a watercress garnish, accompanied by
   the sauce.

Soy & Ginger Fillet Steaks
Serves 6

A very special dinner party dish with an oriental flavour. Serve with boiled rice or noodles and a salad. Excellent on a winter's evening.

Preparation time: 10 mins
Cooking time: 11–13 mins

50g (2oz) butter
10ml (2 teaspoons) corn oil
6 fillet steaks
30ml (2 tablespoons) plain flour
200ml (7 fl oz) red wine
15ml (1 tablespoon) dry sherry
200ml (7 fl oz) beef stock

15ml (1 tablespoon) soy sauce
5ml (1 teaspoon) grated root ginger
Salt and freshly ground black pepper
30ml (2 tablespoons) whipping cream

To garnish
freshly chopped parsley

1. Heat butter and oil in a large frying pan until foaming.
2. Add steaks and cook quickly on each side to seal and brown, then reduce temperature and cook for about 5–7 minutes each side, until steaks are cooked to your liking. Remove and keep warm.
3. Stir flour into pan juices and cook for 1 minute.
4. Stir in the wine, sherry, stock, soy sauce and ginger. Season lightly with salt and pepper. Bring to the boil, stirring. Simmer for 5 minutes.
5. Stir cream into sauce. Re-heat briefly but do not boil.
6. Arrange the steaks on an attractive serving dish and pour over the sauce to serve, garnished with the freshly chopped parsley.

Beef Stir-fry
Serves 6

This Chinese-style recipe is delicious served on a bed of wholemeal noodles. Make sure you have everything prepared before you start to cook.

Preparation time: 15 mins
Cooking time: 11 mins

30ml (2 tablespoons) sunflower oil
1 clove garlic, crushed (optional)
750g (1¹/₂lb) lean rump steak, cut into thin strips

For the sauce

Juice of 2 large oranges, about 175ml (6 fl oz)
2 Chinese stock cubes, dissolved in 85ml (3 fl oz) boiling water .

225g (8oz) dwarf green beans, trimmed and halved
100g (4oz) bean sprouts
225g (8oz) spring cabbage, shredded finely, discarding any stalk

10ml (2 teaspoons) cornflour
1 large orange, segmented without pith or peel

1. Heat the oil in a wok. Add garlic and beef and stir-fry for 3–4 minutes.
2. Add the beans with the bean sprouts and cabbage.
3. Continue to stir-fry for a further 3–4 minutes.
4. Meanwhile, place the orange juice, stock and cornflour in a jug and blend thoroughly.
5. Add the blended ingredients for the sauce to the wok. Cook, stirring, for about 1 minute, until sauce boils and thickens. Stir in the orange segments and heat through. Serve immediately.

Real American Beef Burgers with Blue Cheese
Serves 6

Home-made burgers are super-quick to make and taste completely different to any commercially produced varieties. These have a hidden cheesy taste which is extremely moreish.

Preparation time: 5 mins
Cooking time: 10 mins

750g (1¹/₂lb) lean minced beef
30ml (2 tablespoons) freshly chopped parsley
5ml (1 teaspoon) Worcestershire sauce

Salt and freshly ground black pepper
50g (2oz) Danish blue cheese, cut into six even cubes
6 burger baps, wholemeal or seed-topped if possible

To serve
mixed salad, relish of choice or blue cheese dressing (see page 130)

1. Lightly grease the grill pan and pre-heat grill to medium high.
2. Put the minced beef into a large mixing bowl.
3. Add parsley, Worcestershire sauce and a seasoning of salt and pepper. Mix well. Form into six even burgers.
4. Make a hole in centre of each burger with your thumb. Insert a square of cheese and mould meat around cheese again, to enclose completely.
5. Grill for about 10 minutes, turning once using a fish slice, until cooked to your liking.
6. Serve warm in the split baps accompanied by the salad and relish, or the blue cheese dressing.

Roast Fillet of Beef with Brandy & Cream Sauce

Serves 6

Fillet of beef is expensive so use this recipe for a very special occasion. Basting is of prime importance for succulent roast beef that will melt in your mouth, so don't imagine you can take a short cut and leave it out. Try to plan your meal so that the joint relaxes for 15 minutes before carving, as it will be more tender and succulent. Serve with Speedy Pan Roast Potatoes on page 62 and the salad on page 53.

Preparation time: 10 mins
Cooking time: 45 mins

1 fillet of beef, about 1kg (2lb)
10ml (2 teaspoons) dry
  mustard powder
50g (2oz) beef dripping
60ml (4 tablespoons) brandy
300ml (10 fl oz) double cream

1. Pre-heat the oven to 475°F (240°C) gas mark 9 for at least 15 minutes.
2. Trim any excess fat from the beef. Tie with string at 2.5 cm (1in) intervals. Place in a small roasting tin or glass ovenproof dish.
3. Sprinkle with the mustard powder, then spread evenly with the dripping.
4. Roast the beef in the centre of the oven for 20 minutes, basting twice.
5. Reduce oven temperature to 425°F (220°C) gas mark 7 and continue to roast for a further 20 minutes for medium beef or 25 minutes for well done.
6. Remove meat from oven. Drain juices into saucepan.
7. Cover beef with a tent of foil and set aside for 15 minutes.
8. Stir brandy into juices in saucepan. Set it alight, then keep off heat until flames have died down.
9. Stir in the cream. Season lightly and re-heat gently until hot but not boiling. Serve the beef in thin slices with the sauce poured over.

Smoked Salmon Roulade
Serves 6

Roulade is very simple to make, yet impressive to serve, particularly when filled with smoked salmon and asparagus. Good presented 'al fresco' with plenty of crunchy salad.

Preparation time: 15 mins
Cooking time: 20 mins

50g (2oz) butter
50g (2oz) plain flour
300ml (10 fl oz) milk
Salt and freshly ground black pepper
50g (2oz) freshly chopped parsley
4 eggs, size 2, separated

150ml (5 fl oz) soured cream
45ml (3 tablespoons) lemon mayonnaise
100g (4oz) smoked salmon pieces, chopped roughly
1 × 411g (14¹/₂oz) can cut asparagus spears, drained

To serve
salad leaf garnish

1. Pre-heat the oven to 375°F (190°C) gas mark 5.
2. Lightly butter a swiss roll tin 23 × 33cm (9 × 13in) and line with greaseproof paper. Grease the greaseproof.
3. Melt butter in a large, non-stick saucepan. Add flour and cook for 1 minute, stirring constantly. Gradually add milk, stirring, and bring to the boil. Stir until a thick sauce results. Remove from heat. Cool for 2–3 minutes. Season lightly, then stir in the parsley.
4. Beat in egg yolks, one at a time.
5. In a clean bowl, whisk egg whites until stiff and fold into sauce with a metal spoon.
6. Pour mixture into prepared tin, tilting to fill corners.
7. Bake for 15–20 minutes until well risen and just firm to the touch.
8. Turn out onto a large sheet of greaseproof paper. Peel off greaseproof paper.

9. Cover with a clean tea towel and allow to cool.
10. Meanwhile, in a mixing bowl blend soured cream into mayonnaise. Spread over cooled roulade.
11. Top evenly with smoked salmon pieces, then add asparagus.
12. Roll up the roulade, using one end of the greaseproof to help you. Transfer to serving plate. Serve immediately with a salad garnish.

Fishy Avocados
Serves 6

Avocados combined with tuna fish and cream, then topped with grated cheese and baked – a mouthwatering dish. Serve with baguettes or crisp, bread rolls. As avocados discolour fairly quickly once cut, it's best to prepare and bake these just before serving. Do not expect the cheese to brown, it's simply meant to melt and add flavour.

Preparation time: 15 mins
Cooking time: 15 mins

6 large, ripe avocados
2 × 200g (7oz) cans tuna fish in oil, drained and flaked
225g (8oz) prawns, defrosted if frozen and roughly chopped
60ml (4 tablespoons) double cream
Salt and freshly ground black pepper
100g (4oz) Cheddar cheese, grated

To garnish
sprigs of coriander

1. Pre-heat the oven to 400°F (200°C) gas mark 6.
2. Halve the avocados and remove the stones.
3. Scoop out flesh with a teaspoon and put it into a large mixing bowl. Reserve shells.
4. Mash the flesh with a fork, adding flaked tuna, prawns and cream. Mix well. Season with a little salt and pepper.
5. Pile avocado and tuna mixture back into shells.
6. Top with grated cheese, then arrange shells in one or two ovenproof dishes.
7. Bake for 15 minutes, until cheese melts.
8. Serve immediately in avocado dishes or on saucers, garnished with the coriander.

Salmon & Prawn Bake
Serves 4–6

This delicious fish dish has a crisp top and is very popular in summer with salad. Useful, too, for winter dinner parties, served with a selection of vegetables. So simple to prepare and cook, yet very special to serve and eat.

Preparation time: 10 mins
Cooking time: 23 mins

1 × 418g (15oz) can red
  salmon
225g (8oz) peeled prawns,
  defrosted if frozen

175g (6oz) frozen sweetcorn
  kernels, defrosted
Juice of ¹/₂ lemon

For the topping

75g (3oz) butter
8 slices wholemeal bread, from
  a large cut loaf, crusts
  removed
25g (1oz) rolled oats

1 clove garlic, crushed
  (optional)
30ml (2 tablespoons) freshly
  chopped parsley
50g (2oz) red Leicester cheese,
  grated

To serve
lemon wedges and whole prawns

1. Pre-heat the oven to 375°F (190°C) gas mark 5.
2. Remove skin and bones from the salmon, then flake into a 2-litre (3¹/₂-pint) oval dish with any liquid from the can.
3. Add the prawns and sweetcorn. Sprinkle lemon juice over.
4. Put the butter into a mixing bowl and microwave on DEFROST for 2–3 minutes, until melted. Alternatively, melt the butter in a large pan over a low heat.
5. Make the bread into crumbs in the food processor.
6. Stir breadcrumbs, oats, garlic, parsley and cheese into butter. Mix well with a fork.

7. Spread the mixture over the fish, to cover completely.
8. Bake for about 20 minutes until crisp and golden.
9. Serve, garnished with the whole prawns, accompanied by the wedges of lemon.

Smoked Salmon & Plaice Rolls with Wine & Herb Sauce

Serves 6

Buy skinned plaice fillets from the fishmonger or supermarket for this pretty dish that tastes as good as it looks. Serve with new potatoes and the broccoli with garlic crumbs on page 65.

Preparation time: 5 mins
Cooking time: 14 mins

6 large plaice fillets, skinned if
*   skin is dark*
100g (4oz) smoked salmon

Freshly ground black pepper
120ml (4 fl oz) dry white wine

To complete the sauce

25g (1oz) butter
284ml (9¹/₂ fl oz) carton single
*   cream*
300ml (10 fl oz) fish or
*   vegetable stock*

15ml (1 tablespoon) cornflour
30ml (2 tablespoons) freshly
*   chopped mixed herbs*
*   (tarragon, chives, parsley*
*   and mint)*

1. Cut the plaice fillets in half, lengthwise. Cut the smoked salmon into strips about the same size as the plaice.
2. Lay the plaice on a chopping board, skin side up.
3. Put a strip of salmon on each piece. Season with plenty of black pepper. Roll up each fillet carefully.
4. Pour the wine into a flameproof casserole. Add the fish rolls, seam side down. Cover with a lid.
5. Bring slowly to boiling point, then leave to simmer for 8–10 minutes, until fish is just cooked.
6. Lift the fish rolls onto a serving dish, using a draining spoon. Set aside to keep warm, covered.
7. Add all remaining ingredients to the casserole. Return to heat and bring to the boil, stirring constantly.
8. Simmer for 1–2 minutes, still stirring. Spoon a little of the sauce over the fish, serving remainder separately.

Crispy-topped Cod with Piquant Sauce
Serves 6

Once prepared, the fish cooks to perfection in the oven in just 10 minutes. Great with new potatoes and baked tomatoes. If you only want to cook for two or four people, use approx. 65g (2½oz) bread, cheese and bacon per person.

Preparation time: 10 mins
Cooking time: 10 mins

6 × 200g (7oz) fillets of cod

1 clove garlic, crushed

For the topping

225g (8oz) soft brown breadcrumbs
225g (8oz) Gruyère cheese, grated

30ml (2 tablespoons) freshly chopped parsley
8 rashers streaky bacon, rinded and diced

For the sauce

25g (1oz) butter
1 small onion, chopped
15ml (1 tablespoon) plain flour
200ml (7 fl oz) vegetable stock
250ml (8 fl oz) dry white wine
30ml (2 tablespoons) tomato ketchup

10ml (2 teaspoons) Worcestershire sauce
Salt and freshly ground black pepper
6 small gherkins, drained and sliced

To garnish
sprigs of watercress

1. Pre-heat the oven to 375°F (190°C) gas mark 5.
2. Rub garlic onto cod.
3. Combine breadcrumbs, cheese, parsley and bacon. Sprinkle over cod.
4. Arrange fish in a greased roasting tin and bake uncovered for 10–12 minutes until crisp and lightly golden.
5. Meanwhile, make the sauce. Melt the butter in a medium saucepan and sauté the onion for 5 minutes, until softened.

Stir in the flour and cook for 1 minute.

6. Stir in the stock with the wine, ketchup and Worcestershire sauce. Bring to the boil, stirring. Simmer for 2–3 minutes.
7. Season to taste with salt and pepper. Add the gherkins.
8. Simmer for a further minute or two, then serve the fish with the sauce and watercress garnish.

Baked Summer Salmon
Serves 6

Pretty pink salmon with orange – ideal for a summer lunch or supper. Serve with new potatoes and steamed asparagus or the Chicory Salad on page 49.

Preparation time: 10 mins
Cooking time: 20 mins, or 7–8 mins by microwave

6 salmon steaks or cutlets
Salt and freshly ground black
  pepper
Juice of ¹/2 large orange

15ml (1 tablespoon) extra
  virgin olive oil
30ml (2 tablespoons) freshly
  chopped parsley

To garnish
fresh segments from a large
  orange

sprigs of watercress

1. Pre-heat the oven to 325°F (170°C) gas mark 3.
2. Arrange the salmon on a large sheet of foil, on a baking sheet. Season lightly with a little salt and pepper.
3. In a small jug or mug, combine orange juice, a seasoning of salt and pepper, the olive oil and the parsley.
4. Pour over salmon. Bring edges of foil up and fold over to form a loose parcel.
5. Bake for 15–20 minutes, until salmon is just cooked.
6. To serve, unwrap parcel, carefully lift salmon onto a warmed serving dish and serve with the cooking juices poured over, with a garnish of fresh orange segments and watercress.

   Alternatively, the salmon may be cooked in the microwave – arrange the fish in a shallow dish. Combine orange juice, seasoning, olive oil and parsley and pour over salmon. Cover and microwave on 100%/FULL power for 7–8 minutes, allow to stand, covered, for 2 minutes before serving.

Mustardy Mussels
Serves 6

This simple dish is ideal for a light lunch or evening meal. Serve with chunks of wholemeal bread to mop up the juices. Cooked mussels are available, out of their shells, in supermarkets in 225g (8oz) packs.

Note: If preferred, cook the mussels yourself – see page 25.

Preparation time: 5 mins
Cooking time: 8 mins

300ml (10 fl oz) dry white wine or cider
10ml (2 teaspoons) wholegrain mustard
1 clove garlic, crushed

15g (1/2oz) butter
10ml (2 teaspoons) cornflour
Freshly ground black pepper
750g (11/2lb) cooked mussels, out of their shells

To serve
30ml (2 tablespoons) freshly chopped parsley

1. Put the white wine or cider, mustard, garlic, butter, cornflour and black pepper into a large saucepan. Bring to the boil, stirring with a balloon whisk.
2. Reduce heat to simmer and add the mussels with any liquid.
3. Cover and return to simmer. Cook gently for 4–5 minutes, until mussels are thoroughly hot.
4. Serve the mussels immediately, sprinkled with the freshly chopped parsley.

Cheese, Onion & Herb Plait
Serves 6

This simple pie has a wonderful flavour and is ideal served warm at buffets, or can be cut in slices and packed for picnics.

Note: For speed, chop the onions and grate the cheese in the food processor. Should you prefer to prepare this pie earlier in the day, chill at end of point 7 until ready to bake.

Preparation time: 15 mins
Cooking time: 20 mins

2 medium onions, finely chopped
1 × 450g (1lb) packet puff pastry, defrosted if frozen
100g (4oz) Lancashire cheese, grated

100g (4oz) mature Cheddar cheese, grated
1 egg, size 2, beaten
5ml (1 teaspoon) dried oregano
Salt and freshly ground black pepper

1. Pre-heat the oven to 425°F (220°C) gas mark 7.
2. Put the onions into a mixing bowl. Cover the bowl with cling film and microwave on 100%/FULL power for 3 minutes. Remove from microwave and set aside while you roll out pastry.
3. Roll pastry out to two rectangles, each measuring approx. 30 × 25cm (12 × 10in). Put one oblong on a dampened baking sheet.
4. Combine the two cheeses. Remove about 15ml (1 tablespoon) of the grated cheese and add remainder to the onion with the beaten egg, reserving a little egg for brushing. Add three-quarters of the oregano. Mix well and season lightly with the salt and pepper.
5. Spoon onto centre of first sheet of pastry, leaving a 1cm (½in) edge. Brush edges with water to moisten.
6. Fold second oblong of pastry in half, lengthways, then make cuts 1cm (½in) apart to within 2cm (¾in) of the edge. Lift this folded sheet onto cheese mixture, then open out to fit over first piece exactly. You can trim off extra bits if it's too large.

7. Seal edges, knock up and flute.
8. Brush all over with remaining egg. Sprinkle with remaining cheese and oregano.
9. Bake for 20 minutes until crisp and golden. Serve warm or cold.

Spinach & Walnut Filo Pie
Serves 6

A crispy Greek-style recipe that disappears fast whenever you serve it. This recipe freezes and re-heats well. Especially good served with a choice of salads.

Preparation time: 20 mins
Cooking time: 35 mins

25g (1oz) butter
1 medium onion, chopped
350g (12oz) oyster
  mushrooms, chopped
450g (1lb) frozen chopped
  spinach leaf
100g (4oz) walnuts, chopped
2 eggs, size 2, beaten
150g (5oz) grated cheese (a
  mixture of crumbled feta and
  grated mature Cheddar)

5ml (1 teaspoon) dried
  oregano
Salt and freshly ground black
  pepper
10 sheets filo pastry – 1 × 275g
  (10oz) packet filo pastry
Olive oil, for brushing
5–10ml (1–2 teaspoons) sesame
  seeds

1. Pre-heat the oven to 375°F (190°C) gas mark 5.
2. Melt the butter in a large saucepan, then sauté the onion for 5 minutes, until softened.
3. Stir in the mushrooms, then the spinach and continue to cook, covered, for 5 minutes, until spinach defrosts. Stir occasionally. Drain off excess liquid.
4. Remove from the heat and stir in the walnuts, eggs and 120g (4½oz) of the cheese with the oregano. Season with salt and pepper.
5. Grease the base and sides of a round or square, loose bottomed tin, about 22 × 6cm (9 × 2½in) deep.
6. Layer five sheets of filo into the bottom of the tin, one at a time (brushing each pastry sheet with a little oil, as you layer), to cover base and sides of tin completely and allowing pastry to overlap sides.
7. Spoon filling into pie case.
8. Cover with remaining sheets of pastry, brushing each one

with oil and covering filling completely. Allow pastry to overlap sides again.

9. Tuck sides neatly towards centre. Brush top with oil, then sprinkle with remaining cheese and sesame seeds.

10. Stand on baking sheet and bake for 20 minutes, then increase heat to 425°F (220°C) gas mark 7 and continue to cook for a further 5 minutes, until crisp and golden. Serve warm.

Note: This pie re-heats well. If re-heating from the refrigerator is necessary, pre-heat oven to 400°F (200°C) gas mark 6 and heat the pie, uncovered, for 35–40 minutes.

Pasta with Broccoli, Walnuts & Anchovies
Serves 6

A somewhat different supper dish. Use the remainder of the tomatoes in a vegetable dish or soup the next day. Serve with warm French bread and plenty of red Italian wine.

Preparation time: 10 mins
Cooking time: 10 mins

550g (1¼lb) quick-cooking spaghetti
5ml (1 teaspoon) olive oil
450g (1lb) broccoli florets
30ml (2 tablespoons) olive oil
1 large onion, chopped
1 clove garlic, crushed
75g (3oz) walnuts, chopped

1 × 50g (2oz) can anchovy fillets, drained and chopped
1½ × 400g (14oz) cans chopped tomatoes with herbs
30ml (2 tablespoons) freshly chopped basil
Salt and freshly ground black pepper
Parmesan cheese, grated

1. Cook the spaghetti in a large pan of boiling water, with the oil, according to directions on the packet (about 5–7 minutes).
2. Steam or cook the broccoli in a covered pan, in about 300ml (10 fl oz) boiling water, for approx. 7 minutes, until just tender.
3. Meanwhile, heat the oil in a large frying pan and sauté the onion and garlic for 5 minutes. Add the walnuts and continue to sauté for 2 minutes.
4. Add the anchovies with the tomatoes and basil and bring to simmering point. Season lightly – you won't need much salt because of the anchovies. Stir in the drained broccoli.
5. Drain the spaghetti and return to saucepan. Pour sauce on immediately. Mix thoroughly and serve on heated plates, topped with plenty of Parmesan.

Pasta with Aubergine, Mushrooms & Ricotta
Serves 4

Try serving this light pasta dish for a quick lunch on the patio when summer just starts to turn into autumn. Delicious with French bread and a green salad.

If time allows, remove any bitter juices from the aubergine using the method described on page 11.

Preparation time: 15 mins
Cooking time: 13 mins

500g (18oz) pasta twists or quills
105ml (7 tablespoons) rape seed oil
1 × 275g (10oz) aubergine, diced
225g (8oz) button mushrooms, sliced
1 clove garlic, crushed
1 × 550g (1¼lb) jar passata
Salt and freshly ground black pepper
45ml (3 tablespoons) freshly chopped basil
225g (8oz) petits pois, defrosted if frozen
1 × 250g (9oz) tub ricotta cheese

1. Cook the pasta in a large pan of lightly salted water, with 5ml (1 teaspoon) oil for 10–12 mins, until 'al dente'. Stir once or twice.
2. Meanwhile, heat 90ml (6 tablespoons) oil in a wok.
3. Add the diced aubergine and stir-fry for 4–5 minutes until golden.
4. Transfer to a plate lined with absorbent kitchen paper, using a draining spoon. Add remaining 15ml (1 tablespoon) oil to pan and heat.
5. Add mushrooms and garlic and sauté gently until softened, (2–3 mins).
6. Return aubergines to the wok, add passata, a seasoning of salt and pepper and the basil. Stir in petits pois.
7. Heat through gently, stirring, until thoroughly hot. Remove from heat.
8. Drain pasta and transfer to large, heated serving dish, or six individual dishes. Top with sauce. Sprinkle evenly with ricotta cheese and serve immediately.

Speedy Pizza Slices
Serves 6

These quick and easy pizzas disappear very quickly and the aroma that pervades the kitchen as they bake is pretty good too. Serve with a mixed salad. Excellent as a quick lunch or supper.

You may like to add stoned black olives and a few drained anchovy fillets to the pizzas before baking.

Preparation time: 10 mins
Cooking time: 10–12 mins

1 large red pepper, seeded and finely chopped
1 large onion, finely chopped (use the food processor)
2 cloves garlic, crushed
10ml (2 teaspoons) dried oregano
6 medium ripe tomatoes, peeled and chopped, discarding seeds and core
100g (4oz) mushrooms, chopped

Salt and freshly ground black pepper
1 large white bloomer loaf
60ml (4 tablespoons) olive oil
100g (4oz) smoked ham, sliced into 5mm (1/4in) strips
75g (3oz) mature Cheddar cheese, grated
25g (1oz) Stilton cheese, grated

To serve
tossed mixed salad

1. Pre-heat the oven to 450°F (230°C) gas mark 8.
2. Put the red pepper into a mixing bowl with the onion, garlic, oregano, tomatoes and mushrooms. Season with a little salt and pepper.
3. Cut six thick slices from the centre of the loaf and arrange them on one or two baking sheets. Brush surface of bread with some of the oil.
4. Divide tomato mixture between bread slices, spreading it over evenly. Top with the ham.

5. Combine the grated cheeses and sprinkle over the pizza slices. Drizzle with remaining oil.
6. Bake for 10–12 minutes, until cheese melts. Serve immediately.
   Note: Use remaining part of the bloomer loaf, next day, made into fresh breadcrumbs for another recipe.

Sauces

Curry Sauce
Serves 6

Most young people love curry sauce. This recipe will hopefully encourage teenagers to make it themselves. Serve with barbecue foods, rice and pasta dishes or with hard-boiled eggs for a 'curry in a flash'.

Preparation time: 10 mins
Cooking time: 25 mins

30ml (2 tablespoons) olive oil
1 large onion, chopped
1 carrot, scrubbed clean and
   diced
1 eating apple, peeled, cored
   and chopped
15ml (1 tablespoon) curry
   powder

25g (1oz) plain flour
5ml (1 teaspoon) curry paste
450ml (15 fl oz) chicken stock
10ml (2 teaspoons) lemon juice
5ml (1 teaspoon) oregano
50g (2oz) sultanas

1. Heat the oil in a large, heavy-based saucepan. Add onion, carrot and apple and sauté for 5 minutes until onion softens.
2. Stir in the curry powder with the flour and paste. Cook, stirring, for 1 minute.
3. Add the stock with the lemon juice and oregano. Bring to the boil, stirring frequently. Stir in sultanas. Simmer, covered, for 20 minutes.
4. Serve immediately or cool, then refrigerate and re-heat later.

Easy Peasy Curry Sauce
Serves 6

An especially easy sauce that tastes surprisingly rich and creamy. Leave simmering for 15–20 minutes for a slightly better flavour if you have time, or make earlier in the day and re-heat gently to serve.

Preparation time: 10 mins
Cooking time: 13 mins

40g (1¹/₂oz) butter
2 medium onions, chopped
25g (1oz) plain flour

10ml (2 teaspoons) medium
*   Madras curry powder*
450ml (³/₄ pint) chicken stock
50g (2oz) sultanas

1. Melt the butter in a medium-sized saucepan. Add onions and cook over a gentle heat for 7 minutes, stirring occasionally.
2. Add flour and curry powder. Continue to cook, stirring, for 2 minutes.
3. Gradually stir in the stock. Bring to the boil, stirring.
4. Cook for 2–3 minutes, stirring, until thickened. Add sultanas and simmer for 10 minutes, then serve.

Barbecue Sauce
Serves 6

A tangy sauce that's good with all barbecue food. Try it with roast chicken and rice dishes, too.

Preparation time: 10 mins
Cooking time: 10–15 mins

30ml (2 tablespoons) olive oil
1 medium onion, chopped
30ml (2 tablespoons) cornflour
30ml (2 tablespoons) golden syrup
30ml (2 tablespoons) red wine vinegar
10ml (2 teaspoons) Worcestershire sauce

15ml (1 tablespoon) soy sauce
30ml (2 tablespoons) tomato purée
2.5ml (1/2 teaspoon) hot chilli powder
450ml (15 fl oz) well flavoured beef stock
Garlic salt

1. Heat the oil in a large pan. Sauté the onion for 5 minutes, until softened.
2. Remove pan from heat. Stir in the cornflour, followed by the golden syrup, red wine vinegar, Worcestershire sauce, soy sauce, tomato purée, chilli powder and the stock. Bring to the boil, stirring.
3. Simmer, uncovered, for 5–10 minutes.
4. Season with the garlic salt, to taste. Serve.

Tomato Salsa
Serves 6

Wonderful served with rice and pasta dishes, also good with savoury pies.

Note: If serving this for the wedding buffet on page 267, the quantity should be trebled.

Preparation time: 5 mins
Cooking time: 0

1 × 400g (14oz) can chopped tomatoes
½ bunch spring onions, chopped
1 small red pepper, seeded and finely chopped
3 cloves garlic, chopped

15ml (1 tablespoon) freshly chopped parsley
90ml (6 tablespoons) olive oil
30ml (2 tablespoons) white wine vinegar
Salt and freshly ground black pepper

1. Turn the tomatoes into a large mixing bowl. Add the spring onions with the red pepper, garlic, parsley, olive oil and vinegar. Stir well to combine.
2. Season to taste with salt and pepper, then set aside for at least 10 minutes for flavours to mingle (or prepare well in advance).
3. Stir again, just before serving.

Asparagus Sauce
Serves 6–8

Serve this creamy sauce with poached or grilled fish, or try it with poultry or pork dishes for real luxury. Pour it over jacket potatoes, adding a topping of grated cheese, or some chopped walnuts maybe, for a quick lunch or supper dish.

Preparation time: 5 mins
Cooking time: 11 mins

350g (12oz) fresh asparagus, chopped into 1.25cm (1in) pieces, discarding woody ends
475ml (16 fl oz) light chicken or vegetable stock
25g (1oz) butter
15ml (1 tablespoon) rape seed oil
1 clove garlic, crushed
50g (2oz) plain flour
300ml (10 fl oz) single cream
Salt and freshly ground black pepper
15ml (1 tablespoon) freshly snipped chives

1. Preferably steam, or simmer the asparagus in the stock if you don't possess a steamer, until just tender (8–10 minutes).
2. Drain asparagus, reserving the stock if used. Set asparagus aside.
3. Put the butter and oil into a medium-sized pan. Heat until butter melts. Remove from heat. Stir in garlic and flour. Stir in stock, gradually. Return to heat.
4. Bring to the boil, stirring, then simmer for 5 minutes. Remove pan from heat.
5. Add cream and heat gently for 2–3 minutes, still stirring; do not boil.
6. Season lightly with salt and pepper. Stir in asparagus and chives. Re-heat gently. Serve immediately.

Blue Cheese Dressing
Serves 6

A tangy dressing that's good with barbecue food and salads, and ideal as a sandwich filling with plenty of crunchy salad. Good as a dip with vegetable sticks, too.

Preparation time: 8 mins
Cooking time: 0

60ml (4 tablespoons) creamy fromage frais
60ml (4 tablespoons) mayonnaise

50g (2oz) blue cheese – Stilton, Danish Blue, etc.
Approx. 85ml (3 fl oz) milk

1. Put the fromage frais in a mixing bowl with the mayonnaise.
2. Grate the blue cheese and stir into the mixing bowl.
3. Gradually blend in the milk to make a soft, creamy dressing.
4. Chill until ready to serve – as the dressing thickens on chilling, you may need to stir in a little more milk on serving.

Tangy Yoghurt Mayonnaise
Serves 6

Preparation time: 5 mins
Cooking time: 0

*1 × 500ml (17 fl oz) jar good
   quality French mayonnaise
150ml (5 fl oz) natural yoghurt
15ml (1 tablespoon) freshly
  chopped tarragon*

*Grated rind of 1 lemon
10ml (2 teaspoons) lemon juice
5ml (1 teaspoon) paprika
  pepper*

1. Put all ingredients into a mixing bowl. Stir with a wooden spoon to blend.
2. Turn into serving dish and cover until ready to serve.

Apricot Sauce
Serves 6

Apricot sauce makes a refreshing change from orange to serve
with duck. Try it also with pheasant and pork, or pour it over
puddings and ice cream.

Preparation time: 5 mins
Cooking time: 5 mins

10ml (2 teaspoons) arrowroot
350ml (12 fl oz) apricot juice
Grated rind of 1/2 orange

10ml (2 teaspoons) clear honey
(optional)

1. Mix the arrowroot with a little of the apricot juice.
2. Put remaining apricot juice into a saucepan with the orange
   rind. Stir in the blended juice.
3. Heat, stirring continuously, until sauce boils and thickens.
   Serve immediately, stirring in the honey, if using.

Strawberry Sauce
Serves 6

Quickly made strawberry sauce is delicious on ice creams and sorbets. It will make fresh fruits such as peaches, raspberries, bananas, apricots and melons into dinner party desserts, and is also good with pancakes.

Preparation time: 5 mins
Cooking time: 6 mins

450g (1lb) fresh strawberries, hulled and roughly chopped
100g (4oz) raspberries or tayberries, hulled
45ml (3 tablespoons) Crème de Cassis
50g (2oz) caster sugar

1. Put the strawberries into a medium-sized pan with the raspberries or tayberries and 60ml (4 tablespoons) water, Crème de Cassis and the sugar.
2. Heat gently until fruit softens and juices run (5 minutes).
3. Turn into food processor and process until smooth, using the metal blade.
4. Pass through a sieve and serve warm or cold. The sauce will thicken slightly on cooling.

Redcurrant Sauce
Serves 6

Transform ice cream or pancakes into super fruity desserts with this tangy sauce. Top the pavlova on page 145 or try serving the Fruity Freezer Pud on page 213 with a jug of this brightly coloured topping.

Preparation time: 5 mins
Cooking time: 0

450g (1lb) redcurrants
Juice of ¹/₂ lemon
30ml (2 tablespoons) caster sugar, or to taste

30ml (2 tablespoons) Cointreau or Grand Marnier

1. Put the redcurrants into the food processor with the lemon juice.
2. Whizz to a purée then sieve. Stir the sugar and the Cointreau or Grand Marnier into the purée. Taste and add a little more sugar if required.
3. Serve in a jug.

Desserts

Redcurrant & Apple Delight
Serves 6

A fruity dessert that is wonderfully refreshing on the palate.
Serve after a rich main course. If preferred, this pud may be
made a day in advance.

Preparation time: 15–20 mins
Cooking time: 6–8 mins + chilling time

750g (1¹/₂lb) cooking apples,
  peeled, cored and sliced
225g (8oz) redcurrants, fresh
  or frozen, removed from
  stem

1 × 135g (4³/₄oz) blackcurrant
  flavoured jelly tablet
75g (3oz) caster sugar
50ml (2 fl oz) medium sweet
  cider

To serve
Greek yoghurt (optional)

To decorate
variegated mint leaves

1. Put the apples and redcurrants into a large saucepan with the
   jelly, snipped up roughly with scissors. Add 150ml (5 fl oz)
   water and the sugar.
2. Stirring occasionally, heat over a medium heat until sugar and
   jelly dissolve.
3. Cover with a lid and cook for about 6–8 minutes, until apples
   are soft. Stir once or twice during cooking.
4. Remove from heat and rub through a sieve, then stir well to
   blend. Stir in the cider.
5. Divide between six wine glasses, filling each one about
   three-quarters full. This is easiest done using a soup ladle.
6. Chill in fridge until set – about 2 hours or overnight.
7. Serve with a dollop of yoghurt, if using, and decorate with
   mint leaves.

Strawberry & Apple Meringue Pie
Serves 6

As a speedier alternative, this dessert could be served without the meringue topping, but let the apple cool before adding the strawberries.

Preparation time: 15 mins
Cooking time: 22 mins

1 × 20cm (8in) ready-made pastry flan case, available from leading supermarkets

750g (1½lb) Bramley cooking apples
50g (2oz) caster sugar
225g (8oz) strawberries, sliced

For the meringue topping

2 egg whites, size 2

100g (4oz) caster sugar

To serve
fromage frais, cream or ice cream

1. Arrange the pastry case on a baking sheet and pre-heat the oven to 375°F (190°C) gas mark 5.
2. If you have a microwave, peel, core and slice the apples into a 1.7 litre (3 pint) mixing bowl with 30ml (2 tablespoons) water. Sprinkle over the sugar, then cover the bowl with cling film and microwave on 100%/FULL power for 6 minutes. Set aside.

   Conventional cooks should put the apples and sugar into a small pan with 30ml (2 tablespoons) water and cook over a low heat, covered and stirring occasionally, until apples soften. Set aside to cool.
3. Put the egg whites into a completely clean mixing bowl and whisk with an electric whisk until stiff and dry.
4. Whisk the sugar into the egg whites, 1 tablespoon at a time, until a stiff meringue results.

5. Beat the apples to a rough purée. Fold in the sliced strawberries and turn into the flan case.
6. Spoon meringue over fruit to cover completely.
7. Bake in the oven for approx. 15 minutes, until golden. Serve warm or cold with fromage frais, cream or ice cream.

Melon & Blackberry Sundaes
Serves 6

These fruity desserts are simplicity itself to create, yet very pretty and refreshing. They're full of fibre so they're good for you, too! Try using loganberries, raspberries or strawberries instead of blackberries for a change.

Preparation time: 10 mins
Cooking time: 0

350g (12oz) blackberries
1 Galia melon, halved and seeded
45ml (3 tablespoons) Crème de Cassis liqueur or port
90ml (6 tablespoons) Greek yoghurt
Grated zest of 1 orange
30ml (6 teaspoons) demerara sugar

1. Turn the blackberries into a large mixing bowl.
2. Holding the melon over the mixing bowl, ball out the flesh using a melon baller. Alternatively, slice the melon, then peel and dice each slice. Add melon flesh to bowl with any juice.
3. Pour the liqueur or port over the fruit and toss fruit lightly to coat.
4. Divide the fruit and juices between six wine glasses.
5. Turn yoghurt into mixing bowl. Fold in the orange rind. Top each dessert with a spoonful of yoghurt and sprinkle with 1 teaspoon of demerara sugar.
6. Serve immediately or set aside for 30–40 minutes before serving. The flavours will be better if desserts are not chilled before serving.

Poires Hélène
Serves 6

Fresh, ripe pears served with ice cream, hot chocolate sauce and nuts make a quick dessert which is pretty moreish. Good in the autumn when British pears are at their best. You will need six glass sundae dishes.

Preparation time: 10 mins
Cooking time: 0

6 firm dessert pears (Williams, if possible)
6 scoops vanilla ice cream or yoghurt ice cream

1 recipe Chocolate Sauce (see page 155), served warm

To decorate
crystallised violets

1. Carefully peel and core the halved pears.
2. Put one scoop of ice cream into each of the sundae dishes. Add two pear halves to each dish.
3. Top with chocolate sauce, then serve immediately, decorated with the crystallised violets.

Chestnut Purée with Raspberries
Serves 6

A rich creamy dessert that's so good with tangy raspberries. You could use frozen raspberries when fresh aren't available. Fresh apricots or strawberries also work well with the chestnuts.

Preparation time: 10 mins
Cooking time: 0

275g (10oz) unsweetened chestnut purée (from a can)
50g (2oz) icing sugar, sieved

30ml (2 tablespoons) medium sherry
300ml (10 fl oz) double cream
350g (12oz) raspberries

1. Turn the chestnut purée into a large mixing bowl. Using a wooden spoon, beat in the icing sugar.
2. In a separate bowl, beat the cream using an electric whisk until it stands in soft peaks.
3. Fold the sherry and cream into the chestnut purée with a metal spoon.
4. Divide the purée between six ramekins.
5. Chill in the fridge for at least 20 minutes. Top with the raspberries and serve.

Apple Pop-overs
Serves 6

Light, crisp desserts which are best served straight from the oven dredged with a little icing sugar. Offer a bowl of Greek yoghurt, tangy crème fraîche or ice-cold vanilla ice cream. Vary the fruit – try stoned cherries, peaches or pears. Also good with roast beef if you omit the sugar. You will need a six-hole muffin pan.

Preparation time: 10 mins
Cooking time: 25 mins

100g (4oz) plain flour
1 egg, size 2
300ml (10 fl oz) semi-skimmed milk
25g (1oz) lard

225g (8oz) Bramley apples, peeled, cored and roughly chopped
7.5ml (1/2 tablespoon) caster sugar

To serve
sifted icing sugar

1. Pre-heat the oven to 425°F (220°C) gas mark 7.
2. Make the batter – put the flour into a mixing bowl, make a well in the centre and add the egg, then gradually add half the milk, beating with a wooden spoon from the centre outwards, to produce a smooth batter.
3. Stir in remaining milk. Set aside for 5 minutes.
4. Divide lard between the muffin pans. Pop into the pre-heated oven until melted and very hot (about 5 minutes).
5. Fold apple into batter, then stir in the caster sugar.
6. Spoon batter evenly into the muffin pan – there should be a sizzle as you add the batter to the hot lard. Quickly return pan to oven.
7. Bake for 20–25 minutes until well risen and golden. Serve immediately topped with a snow of sifted icing sugar.

Autumn Pudding
Serves 6–8

Although this dessert needs to stand for 3–4 hours before serving, it is quick and easy to assemble and can be refrigerated overnight if preferred. Serve this ever-popular pud with Greek yoghurt, ice cream or crème fraîche. It's very easy to cut and serve this dessert if you use a loaf pan. Frozen soft fruits, defrosted first, work well in this recipe if you can't get fresh. You will need a 1.2 litre (2 pint) pudding basin or loaf pan.

Preparation time: 15 mins + standing time
Cooking time: 0

*275g (10oz) brown sliced
    bread*
75g (3oz) caster sugar
150ml (5 fl oz) red wine

*1.25kg (2¹/₂lb) fresh autumn
    fruits (cooking apples,
    pears, redcurrants,
    loganberries, blackberries,
    blackcurrants, plums)*

To decorate
sprigs of fresh mint

*a few strawberries or sprigs of
    blackcurrants*

1. Remove crusts from the bread, then use 200g (7oz) to line the base and sides of the pudding basin or loaf pan.
2. In a large saucepan, dissolve the sugar in the wine over a low heat.
3. Prepare the fruit. Peel and core the apples and pears, then chop roughly. Add to the pan with the rest of the fruit.
4. Simmer the fruit for 8–10 minutes, until soft.
5. Drain the fruit, reserving the juice. Spoon into basin or loaf pan, then make a lid out of remaining bread to cover fruit completely.
6. Place a saucer or cling film on top of pudding and a weight, such as a can of baked beans or tin of syrup. Chill for 3–4 hours or overnight if more convenient.
7. Turn pud out onto a dish. Pour over the reserved juice. Decorate with a sprig of mint and a few fruits.

Strawberries with Orange Juice
Serves 6

When English strawberries are available in June and July, there
is simply no better sweet. Try this orangey version which is so
quick and easy, yet makes a special dessert that's popular with all
age groups and suitable for all sorts of entertaining.

Note: You could use Kirsch, Grand Marnier or Cointreau
instead of the orange juice, if preferred.

Preparation time: 5 mins + standing time
Cooking time: 0

750g (1¹/₂lb) ripe strawberries
22.5ml (1¹/₂ tablespoons) caster
sugar

45ml (3 tablespoons) orange
juice

To serve
whipped cream, Greek yoghurt or crème fraîche

1. Hull and thickly slice the strawberries. Layer into a glass
   serving bowl, sprinkling with the sugar as you go.
2. Pour the orange juice over the strawberries, then cover the
   bowl and set aside for 15 minutes for flavours to mingle.
3. Serve with cream, Greek yoghurt or crème fraîche.

Fresh Fruit Brûlée
Serves 6

Crème fraîche is a delicious, thick, soured cream from France. Try different fruits in this super dessert, such as raspberries, redcurrants, grapes or bananas. Brandy snaps are readily available in supermarkets.

Preparation time: 10 mins
Cooking time: 2–3 mins + 40 mins chilling time

450g (1lb) strawberries, washed and sliced
2 ripe nectarines, washed and chopped

4 brandy snap biscuits, crushed
1 × 500ml (17 fl oz) carton crème fraîche
200g (7oz) demerara sugar

1. Put the strawberries and nectarines into a 1.5 litre (2½ pint) oval dish.
2. Sprinkle the brandy snaps over the fruit.
3. Spoon over the crème fraîche to cover the fruit and biscuits completely. Chill in the fridge for at least 40 minutes.
4. Sprinkle over the sugar evenly, to cover the crème fraîche completely.
5. When ready to serve, put the dish under a pre-heated hot grill for about 5 minutes, until the sugar melts and caramelises. Watch carefully as it suddenly turns.
6. Serve immediately. The contrast of the warm crisp topping and cold cream and fruit is sensational.

Raspberry Pavlova with Redcurrant Sauce
Serves 6

Although pavlova takes time in the oven, it is so quick to make and to assemble afterwards. It makes a truly dramatic sweet that is almost everyone's favourite. Make the base a day in advance, if preferred.

Preparation time: 15 mins
Cooking time: 1 hour 15 mins

3 egg whites, size 2
175g (6oz) caster sugar
5ml (1 teaspoon) vinegar
5ml (1 teaspoon) cornflour
5ml (1 tablespoon) almond
   nibs or chopped nuts

300ml (10 fl oz) whipping
   cream, whipped
225g (8oz) raspberries and
   redcurrants, mixed
2 passion fruits, seeds only

Serve with
redcurrant sauce (see page 134)

1. Pre-heat the oven to 300°F (150°C) gas mark 2.
2. Lightly grease a baking sheet and line with baking parchment on which you have drawn a 20cm (8in) circle on the under-side. Do not grease the parchment.
3. Put the egg whites into a clean, grease-free bowl and beat, using an electric whisk, until stiff and dry.
4. Gradually whisk in the sugar a tablespoon at a time, until a stiff, glossy meringue results.
5. Blend together the vinegar and cornflour and fold into the meringue swiftly, using a metal spoon.
6. Spread mixture out to cover the circle on the baking parch-ment, building up the sides so that they are slightly higher than the centre. Sprinkle nuts over sides.
7. Put meringue into oven, near the top, turn oven down immediately to 275°F (140°C) gas mark 1. Leave for 1 hour 15 minutes – do not open oven door. Then turn oven off and leave meringue in the oven to cool. It can be left overnight.

8. Remove from oven. Peel off baking parchment and arrange on flat serving plate.
9. Spread whipped cream over centre of pavlova. Top with fruit. Spoon over passion fruit seeds and serve within 1 hour if possible.

Fruit Salad Stunner
Serves 6

A refreshing dessert which looks spectacular yet is quick to prepare. Excellent for summer supper parties and pretty on a buffet table, too.

Preparation time: 15 mins
Cooking time: 0

1 cantaloupe melon
225g (8oz) strawberries, halved
1 kiwi fruit, peeled and sliced
100g (4oz) dark cherries,
  stoned

100g (4oz) seedless white
  grapes
30ml (2 tablespoons) Kirsch

To serve
whipped cream or Greek yoghurt

1. Cut the melon in half, then scoop out seeds and discard. Scoop out and dice the flesh, retaining the melon skins. Put melon into a large mixing bowl with any juice.
2. Add the strawberries, kiwi fruit, cherries and grapes.
3. Pour Kirsch over the fruit. Toss lightly.
4. Serrate edges of melon halves with scissors, if you have time, to make them look pretty.
5. Pile prepared fruit back into melon halves and serve with a bowl of whipped cream or Greek yoghurt.

Rhubarb Fool
Serves 6–8

A truly English dessert. There are many, many recipes for rhubarb fool – this one is light and summery. If you prefer a richer dessert, use whipped double cream instead of yoghurt and if you want to be ultra-healthy, use fromage frais; all work equally well with the rhubarb.

Preparation time: 10 mins
Cooking time: 15–20 mins

1kg (2lb) rhubarb
100g (4oz) caster sugar, or to taste
275g (10oz) Greek yoghurt

100g (4oz) almond macaroon biscuits, each one cut into 4 pieces

1. Cut the rhubarb into chunks and put them into a large saucepan with the sugar and 30ml (2 tablespoons) water.
2. Cover the pan with a lid and cook the rhubarb very gently for 15–20 minutes, stirring fairly frequently, until tender but not mushy.
3. Put the rhubarb into a sieve over a mixing bowl to drain off a little of the liquid.
4. Turn the drained rhubarb into another mixing bowl and mash with a fork until smooth. Allow to cool completely.
5. Stir the yoghurt and the macaroon biscuits into the cold rhubarb.
6. Turn into wine glasses and chill until ready to serve.

Sherry Banana Splits
Serves 6

Ripe bananas with dairy ice cream and sherry – a perfect combination of luxury and flavours! Do make sure the bananas are really ripe for this recipe, but not over ripe and squidgy. The sherry is served in glasses beside the splits.

Preparation time: 10 mins
Cooking time: 0

6 medium-sized ripe bananas
12 scoops of vanilla ice cream
100g (4oz) toasted flaked almonds
3 chocolate flakes

Dark chocolate or maple syrup ice cream topping
6 ice cream fan wafers
6 sherry glasses of pale cream sherry, such as Amontillado

1. Peel and split bananas.
2. Put two scoops of ice cream into each long sundae dish. Arrange bananas either side of ice cream. Sprinkle with the flaked almonds.
3. Break each chocolate flake in half, then crumble half a flake over each dessert.
4. Squirt a little topping over desserts and decorate with a wafer.
5. Serve the desserts immediately with a glass of sherry.

Bubbly Jelly with Apricots & Peaches
Serves 6

This pretty dessert tastes refreshing and summery whenever it's served. Popping it into the freezer for 30 minutes helps it to set more quickly. You could serve the desserts in individual wine glasses or ramekins. Serve with any fresh fruit in season.

Preparation time: 10 mins
Cooking time: 2 mins

1 × 411g (14¹/₂oz) can apricot halves in syrup, drained
1 × 142g (4¹/₂oz) tablet of good quality orange jelly
Lemonade – see method

1 × 200ml (7 fl oz) carton crème fraîche
3 fresh peaches, sliced, or 225g (8oz) strawberries, sliced

1. Put the apricots into the base of a 1.2 litre (2 pint) glass jelly mould or oblong terrine dish.
2. Break the jelly into cubes and place them in a large heatproof measuring jug with 90ml (6 tablespoons) cold water. Microwave for 1¹/₂ minutes on 100%/FULL power. Stir to dissolve – if jelly has not dissolved after stirring, microwave for a further 30 seconds, then stir again.

3. Stir in sufficient lemonade to bring the level on the jug up to 600ml (1 pint).
4. Pour jelly carefully over apricots. Chill in the fridge until set.
5. To serve, turn jelly out onto serving dish (dip the mould into hot water and count to 10 first).
6. Carefully stir the crème fraîche, then spread it all over the top of the jelly. Decorate with the peaches or strawberries and serve immediately.

Lemon Snow
Serves 6

Serve this refreshing, light dessert in pretty sundae dishes or wine glasses. Brandy snaps or chocolate wafers are delicious with the tangy apples in this pud. Try whisking egg whites in a 1 litre (1¾ pint) jug – it's quick and easy.

Preparation time: 10 mins
Cooking time: 9 mins + chilling time

1kg (2lb) Bramley apples,
  peeled, cored and sliced
Grated rind of 1 lemon

Juice of 2 lemons
100g (4oz) caster sugar
3 egg whites, size 2

To decorate
6 single strands of redcurrants or 6 strawberries

To serve
brandy snaps or chocolate wafers

1. Put apples into a large saucepan with the rind and juice of the lemons.
2. Cover with a lid and cook over a gentle heat until apples soften. Alternatively, if you have a microwave, put apples and lemon juice into a large mixing bowl. Cover and microwave on 100%/FULL power for 8–9 minutes.
3. Stir in sugar and beat to a purée. Set pan in a bowl or sink of ice cold water, to come three-quarters up the sides. Leave to cool completely.
4. In a large clean bowl or glass jug, whisk egg whites until they stand in soft peaks. Fold into apple mixture with a metal spoon.
5. Divide between six sundae dishes or wine glasses and decorate each one with the redcurrants or strawberries. Chill for 10 minutes or until ready to serve. Serve with brandy snaps or chocolate wafers.

Fresh Strawberry Dippers
Serves 6

Strawberries are now readily available for about nine months of the year. Serve these dippers either for dessert or as petits fours. They are always very popular. You will need some sweet paper cases.

Preparation time: 10 mins
Cooking time: 5 mins

450g (1lb) whole strawberries with calyx intact

175g (6oz) plain chocolate, broken into pieces

1. Wash and dry strawberries on absorbent kitchen paper.
2. Put chocolate into a medium-sized mixing bowl and set this over a pan of simmering water, stirring often, until chocolate melts. Remove bowl from heat.
3. Dip half of each strawberry into chocolate, then arrange on non-stick baking parchment. Leave to set.
4. Serve in sweet paper (petits fours) cases.

Caramelised Oranges & Grapefruit
Serves 6

Citrus fruit with caramel is a super combination. The easiest way to make the caramel is in the microwave, but make sure you use a large heatproof jug with a handle as the caramel gets very hot. Serve with Greek yoghurt or crème fraîche. This dessert can be made the day before, if preferred.

Preparation time: 15 mins
Cooking time: 15 mins + chilling time

4 large oranges
2 pink grapefruit
30ml (2 tablespoons) Kirsch or
* Grand Marnier*

Approx. 20g (³/₄oz) crystallised
* ginger in syrup, drained and*
* chopped*
175g (6oz) caster sugar

1. Peel one orange thinly, taking care not to remove any pith.
2. Cut the peel into thin strips and blanch in a small pan of boiling water for 2 minutes. Drain and put into a small bowl. Just cover with cold water and reserve.
3. Peel remaining oranges and grapefruit, removing all pith. Remove pith from the first orange.
4. Slice the fruits thinly or segment the fruits, discarding pips but reserving any juice that results.
5. Arrange the fruit with any juice in a shallow serving dish. Pour liqueur over fruit. Sprinkle over the ginger.
6. Put the sugar and 120ml (4 fl oz) water into a 1 litre (1³/₄ pint) heatproof jug and microwave on 100%/FULL power for 9–13 minutes, until a dark golden caramel results. Watch carefully as microwave ovens vary in the time this will take. Do not stir at all. Use oven gloves to remove jug carefully from microwave.
7. Pour the caramel over the fruit immediately.
8. Chill until ready to serve (allow at least 40 minutes). Drain orange rind and sprinkle over caramelised oranges on serving.

Raspberry & Orange Compote with Hot Chocolate Sauce

Serves 6

A refreshing dessert that looks pretty and tastes out of this world. Serve with fromage frais or single cream. Try varying the fruits – pink grapefruit and redcurrants are good, and so are pears with oranges and strawberries. Make the sauce in advance if preferred and re-heat to serve. Can also be served cold.

Preparation time: 15 mins
Cooking time: 5 mins

5 large oranges　　　　　　*25g (1oz) caster sugar*
350g (12oz) raspberries

For the sauce

15ml (1 tablespoon) cornflour　　*15g (1/2oz) butter*
100g (4oz) plain chocolate

1. Remove peel and pith from the oranges, holding the fruit over a bowl to catch the drips.
2. Segment oranges and divide evenly between six sundae dishes. Pour over any reserved juice.
3. Hull the raspberries, wash and dry if necessary and add to the oranges. Sprinkle with the sugar.
4. Make the sauce. Measure 300ml (10 fl oz) water in a jug. In a medium-sized non-stick pan, blend the cornflour to a smooth paste with a little of the water. Stir in remaining water.
5. Break the chocolate into pieces and add to the pan with the butter.
6. Bring mixture slowly to the boil, stirring. Cook for about 1 minute, stirring.
7. Serve the fruit immediately with a little of the hot sauce poured over.

Raspberry & Peach Creams
Serves 6

A light dessert that can be made and served very quickly. Vary the fruits when raspberries and peaches are not in season. Try strawberries with bananas, pears with apple and a little freshly grated root ginger, or loganberries with oranges.

Preparation time: 15 mins
Cooking time: 0

150ml (5 fl oz) double cream
200g (7oz) creamy fromage frais
15ml (1 tablespoon) caster sugar, or to taste

Finely grated rind of 1 orange
30ml (2 tablespoons) Cointreau or Grand Marnier
350g (12oz) raspberries
2 large, ripe peaches

To serve
6 crisp wafer biscuits

1. In a large mixing bowl, whip the cream until standing in soft peaks. Fold in the fromage frais with the caster sugar, half the orange rind and the liqueur.
2. Put raspberries into a large mixing bowl.
3. Put peaches into a bowl and pour boiling water over them. Allow to stand for 1 minute, then plunge into cold water. (The skins will then be very easy to peel off.)
4. Halve the peeled peaches, remove stones, then slice the flesh and add to the raspberries.
5. Layer the cream into six wine glasses.
6. Top with the mixed fruits. Sprinkle each dessert with a little orange rind and decorate with a wafer.
7. Serve immediately or chill the desserts, without the wafers, until ready to serve.

Chocolate Orange Pots
Serves 6

Some people may prefer to eat the chocolate mousse without the cream topping. Plain chocolate orange with its unique flavour makes a wonderful rich pud. The cream topping is flavoured with Cointreau and the desserts are decorated with slices of fresh orange to continue the theme. You will need six ramekin dishes.

Preparation time: 10 mins
Cooking time: 5 mins

1 × 200g (7oz) plain chocolate orange

25g (1oz) butter
4 eggs, size 2

To decorate (optional)

150ml (5 fl oz) double cream
15ml (1 tablespoon) Cointreau

1 orange

1. Break up the chocolate orange and put it into a large mixing bowl. Add the butter.
2. Melt the chocolate over a pan of simmering water, stirring frequently. Remove bowl from pan. Alternatively, put the bowl into the microwave and microwave on Power 4/SIMMER for 4–5 minutes, until melted. Stir every 2 minutes.
3. Separate eggs, putting egg whites into a clean mixing bowl. Beat the yolks, one at a time, into the melted chocolate. Beat well until smooth.
4. Whisk egg whites until stiff, then fold them into the mixture lightly and evenly, using a metal spoon.
5. Divide the chocolate mousse mixture between the ramekins. Chill until set.
6. When ready to serve, whip the cream until stiff, fold in the liqueur then spoon the cream onto the desserts.
7. Peel and segment the orange, discarding pith and membrane.
8. Serve each dessert topped with a slice of orange. As an alternative, serve the chocolate pots with the strawberries with orange juice on page 143.

Syllabub
Serves 6

Serve this creamy dessert with special ice cream wafers or brandy snaps. Supermarkets sell excellent biscuits or you could make your own as they keep well in an airtight tin. Try the easy biscuits recipe on page 173.

Preparation time: 5 mins
Cooking time: 0

*150ml (5 fl oz) fruity medium
   white wine
Juice and rind of 1 large
   lemon, strained*

*50g (2oz) caster sugar
300ml (10 fl oz) double cream*

To decorate
seedless grapes

1. Put all the ingredients into a mixing bowl and whisk, using an electric whisk, until holding its shape.
2. Spoon into stemmed wine glasses and chill for at least 10 minutes before serving, topped with 3 grapes per glass.

Strawberries & Cream Mousse
Serves 6–8

The perfect summer combination of strawberries and cream are used here to make a perfect mousse. A light dessert to serve often now that strawberries are more frequently available in supermarkets. This dessert freezes well.

Preparation time: 15 mins
Cooking time: 2–3 mins

1 × 11g (0.4oz) packet gelatine
450g (1lb) strawberries
30ml (2 tablespoons) Crème de Cassis

3 eggs, size 2, separated
75g (3oz) caster sugar
450ml (15 fl oz) double cream

To decorate
fresh strawberries   *strawberry leaves, if available*

1. Put 60ml (4 tablespoons) water into a small heatproof bowl and sprinkle over the gelatine. Set aside for 5–6 minutes.
2. Hull and halve the strawberries and put into the food processor, using the metal blade. Add Crème de Cassis, egg yolks and sugar. Process until puréed. Pass through a sieve into a large bowl.
3. In a clean bowl, whip cream until floppy and fold into strawberry mixture.
4. In another clean bowl, whip egg whites until stiff.
5. Dissolve gelatine over a pan of simmering water, stirring, or alternatively, dissolve gelatine on SIMMER in the microwave – this should take 2–3 minutes, stir every minute.
6. Fold dissolved gelatine, then egg whites into strawberry mixture using a metal spoon.
7. Turn into a pretty glass dish and refrigerate until set. Serve the dessert decorated with the strawberries and strawberry leaves.

Chocolate, Apricot & Ginger Ice Cream
Serves 6

Serve this sumptuous dessert with a jug of the apricot sauce on page 132. Crush the biscuits by putting them in a strong plastic bag and crushing with a rolling pin.

Preparation time: 15 mins + freezing time
Cooking time: 0

75g (3oz) dried apricots,
  roughly chopped
Rind and juice of 1 orange
1 litre (1³/4 pints) vanilla ice
  cream

100g (4oz) dark chocolate,
  chopped roughly
100g (4oz) ginger biscuits,
  crushed roughly

1. Put the dried apricots into a bowl. Add the rind and juice of the orange and set aside for 15 minutes (or up to 2 hours, if preferred).
2. Turn ice cream into a chilled mixing bowl. Mash with a fork to soften slightly.
3. Mix in the apricots and orange juice, the chocolate and ginger biscuits, working fairly quickly so that the ice cream doesn't melt too much.
4. Turn into a 1.1 litre (2 pint) pudding basin. Cover and freeze until firm.
5. To serve, dip briefly in hot water to unmould, then turn onto cold serving plate. Transfer to fridge for 30 minutes before serving.

Fruity Yoghurt Ice Cream
Serves 6

A refreshing fruity standby to have in the freezer, all ready for unexpected guests. Remove from freezer and allow the ice cream to stand in the fridge for 30 minutes before serving to bring out the true flavours.

Preparation time: 15 mins + freezing time
Cooking time: 0

450g (1lb) Greek strained
  yoghurt
450g (1lb) summer fruits
  (raspberries, blackcurrants,
  redcurrants, strawberries)

30ml (2 tablespoons) icing
  sugar
10ml (2 teaspoons) lemon juice
3 egg whites, size 3

1. Turn the yoghurt into a large mixing bowl.
2. Purée the fruits in a food processor, then pass through a sieve if the fruits have pips or seeds.
3. Fold the purée into the yoghurt with the icing sugar and lemon juice.
4. In a large clean bowl, whisk the egg whites until stiff. Fold into the yoghurt mixture.
5. Pour into suitable container and freeze for at least 3 hours. Transfer to refrigerator for 30 minutes before serving.

Meringue Nests
Serves 6

Meringue nests can be prepared or brought well in advance. Store in an airtight container. They make a perfect no-fuss dessert for quick and easy dinner parties.

Preparation time: 10 mins
Cooking time: 0

6 ready-made meringue nests
300ml (10 fl oz) double cream
15ml (1 tablespoon) caster sugar
Grated rind of 1 orange
100g (4oz) loganberries

100g (4oz) strawberries
100g (4oz) redcurrants
1 kiwi fruit, peeled and sliced
30ml (2 tablespoons) orange juice

To decorate
sprigs of fresh mint

1. Arrange meringue nests on six individual serving plates.
2. Whip the cream and caster sugar together until just stiff. Fold in the orange rind, then spoon cream into meringue nests.
3. Put the washed fruit into a mixing bowl and spoon over the orange juice.
4. Arrange fruit on the meringue nests. Decorate with sprigs of mint and serve.

Cherry Filo Purses
Serves 6–8 (makes approx. 8 purses)

Crispy filo pastry filled with cherry pie filling, then brushed with lemon-flavoured butter and baked until crisp – a delicious dessert. Serve warm or cold.

Preparation time: 15 mins
Cooking time: 10–15 mins

15ml (1 tablespoon) lemon juice
50g (2oz) butter
1 × 275g (10oz) packet filo pastry

1 × 400g (14oz) can red cherry pie filling
About 1 dessertspoonful caster sugar

To serve
sifted icing sugar

whipped cream or crème fraîche

1. Pre-heat the oven to 400°F (200°C) gas mark 6.
2. Heat the lemon juice and butter together gently in a saucepan until butter melts. Alternatively, put lemon juice and butter into a small bowl and microwave for about 2 minutes on DEFROST.
3. Lay filo sheets opened out on a worktop in a single stack. Keep them covered with a damp cloth when not actually using.
4. Cut the sheets in half, widthways, right through the stack.
5. Take one half sheet of filo. Arrange another half sheet on top, to form a cross. Lay a third sheet on top to make a third arm, crossing in centre. Brush all over with a little of the lemon butter.
6. Put one good teaspoonful of pie filling in centre of pastry. Pinch up ends and squeeze to form a 'Dick Whittington' type bundle, or purse. Arrange on greased baking sheet.
7. Repeat until all pastry and pie filling have been used.

8. Brush all over with the lemon butter. Sprinkle with the sugar.
9. Bake for 10–15 minutes until golden.
10. Serve warm, dusted with a little sifted icing sugar, with a bowl of cream or crème fraîche.

Baked Alaska
Serves 6

A layer of sponge topped with fruit and a block of ice cream, enclosed in crisp meringue with a gooey centre – naughty but nice! A little of this rich dessert goes a long way. It must be served immediately it is removed from the oven, so you will have to complete it between courses. If you can't find an 18cm (7in) sponge in the supermarket, use a packet of trifle sponges.

Preparation time: 15 mins
Cooking time: 5 mins

18cm (7in) round sponge cake, either home-made or bought from the supermarket
1 × 300g (11oz) can peach slices or apricot halves, in natural juice

3 egg whites, size 2
175g (6oz) caster sugar
1 × 450ml (15 fl oz) block of vanilla ice cream, frozen solid

To serve
single cream

1. Pre-heat the oven to 450°F (230°C) gas mark 8.
2. Put the sponge onto a flat ovenproof dish and spoon over just enough of the juice from the can of fruit to moisten.
3. In a clean mixing bowl, whisk the egg whites until stiff, using an electric whisk.
4. Beat in the sugar a dessertspoonful at a time, continuing to whisk until a stiff meringue results.
5. Put the frozen ice cream in the centre of the sponge and top evenly with the drained fruit.
6. Pile the meringue over the dessert, enclosing fruit, ice cream and cake completely.
7. Pop into the oven for about 3–5 minutes or until the outside of the meringue is lightly browned.
8. Serve immediately, cut into slices, accompanied by single cream.

Banoffi Pie
Serves 6

One of the most frequently requested dessert recipes in restaurants. This easy version works every time, but beware of the calories!

Preparation time: 10 mins
Cooking time: 10 mins + cooling time

75g (3oz) butter
125g (5oz) crushed digestive
    biscuits

1 × 397g (14oz) can sweetened
    condensed milk
175g (6oz) butter
175g (6oz) caster sugar

To decorate
2 ripe bananas or 225g (8oz)
    fresh strawberries, sliced
lemon juice

fine strips of lime peel,
    blanched

To serve
single cream

1. Melt the butter in a large saucepan over a gentle heat.
2. Mix the crushed digestives into the melted butter.
3. Press the mixture into the base and sides of a greased 20cm (8in) loose-bottomed cake tin. Chill in fridge.
4. Pour the condensed milk into a non-stick saucepan. Add the butter and the sugar.
5. Stir over a low heat until the butter melts and the sugar dissolves, then boil for 5 minutes, stirring constantly, to make a light golden caramel.
6. Pour into the biscuit crust and set aside to cool for about 20 minutes.
7. Remove from flan tin and set on serving plate.
8. Slice bananas thinly and sprinkle all over with lemon juice. Arrange over the caramel. Alternatively, slice strawberries and arrange on caramel.
9. Decorate with blanched lime peel and serve immediately.

Almond Meringue Peaches
Serves 6

If you can't get ripe peaches for this dessert, use canned peach halves in natural juice, well drained and blotted dry on absorbent kitchen paper. *Note:* If there's any danger of the peaches falling over, prop them up with crumpled foil.

Preparation time: 12 mins
Cooking time: 15 mins

3 large, ripe peaches
30ml (2 tablespoons) cranberry
*   sauce*
30ml (2 tablespoons) Crème de
*   Cassis*

2 egg whites, size 2
100g (4oz) caster sugar
25g (1oz) ground almonds

To decorate
sifted cocoa powder for
*   sprinkling*

6 strawberries, fanned

To serve
Greek yoghurt or fromage frais

1. Pre-heat the oven to 400°F (200°C) gas mark 6.
2. Halve the peaches, discarding central stone. Place hollow sides up on a baking sheet.
3. Fill each hollow with 5ml (1 teaspoon) cranberry sauce. Drizzle the Crème de Cassis evenly over cranberry sauce on each peach half.
4. Put the egg whites into a large, clean mixing bowl. Whisk until stiff, using an electric mixer.
5. Whisk in the sugar, a dessertspoonful at a time. Continue whisking until a smooth, glossy meringue results. Fold in the ground almonds with a metal spoon.
6. Swirl meringue over each peach half, dividing it evenly.
7. Bake for 10–15 minutes or until lightly browned. Serve warm or cold, dusted with a smidgen of cocoa powder and decorated with a strawberry fan, accompanied by Greek yoghurt or fromage frais.

Chocolate Sponges with Fruit
Serves 6

These light sponges bake to perfection in only 8–10 minutes. Simply delicious with creamy fromage frais and fresh summer fruits. If you can't get fresh fruits, use canned mandarin oranges or apricots, well drained. The mixture will make 12 sponges.

Preparation time: 15 mins
Cooking time: 8 mins

75g (3oz) caster sugar
3 eggs, size 2
50g (2oz) plain flour

25g (1oz) cocoa powder
Caster sugar, for dusting

For the filling

90ml (6 tablespoons) creamy
    fromage frais
350g (12oz) strawberries,
    sliced

About 15ml (1 tablespoon)
    sifted icing sugar

1. Grease and lightly flour 12 patty tins (jam tart tins).
2. Pre-heat the oven to 375°F (190°C) gas mark 5.
3. Put the caster sugar and eggs into a mixing bowl and set the bowl over a pan of hot water, but don't allow bowl to touch the water. Whisk, using a hand-held electric whisk, until the mixture is thick, pale and creamy. This will take about 7–8 minutes.
4. Sieve the flour and cocoa powder together. Using a metal tablespoon, fold in the flour and cocoa powder quickly and evenly.
5. Divide mixture between the patty tins. Sprinkle lightly with caster sugar.
6. Cook in the oven for 6–8 minutes, until well risen and just firm to the touch. Transfer to cooling rack.
7. Arrange one cooled sponge, right way up, in each of six sundae dishes or fruit bowls. Top each with a spoonful of fromage frais.

8. Arrange the sliced fruit on the sponges, putting some to the side if necessary.

9. Add remaining sponges, right side up to form towers. Dust tops of each tower with sifted icing sugar. Serve immediately.

Pain au Chocolat
Serves 6 (makes 6 pains au chocolat)

As good as you get in France and quick and easy to make. Serve with a cup of tea or coffee at tea-time. Ideal for a quick dessert or with brunch or breakfast. Children love these yummy pastries.

Pillsbury French style croissants are part of the range of Pillsbury dough ready-to-bake products available from the chill counter of your local supermarket.

Preparation time: 10 mins
Cooking time: 19–24 mins

1 × 308g (11¼oz) tube
Pillsbury French-style
croissants

12 squares from a bar of plain
chocolate

1. Pre-heat the oven to 375°F (190°C) gas mark 5.
2. Remove dough as indicated and gently separate at perforations to form 6 triangles.
3. Put 2 squares of chocolate, side by side, about 2.5cm (1in) from the end of shortest side of each triangle.
4. Starting at shortest side, roll each piece of croissant dough loosely towards opposite point, as indicated on pack.

5. Place rolls, point side down, on an ungreased baking sheet; curve ends inward to form crescent shapes.
6. Bake in pre-heated oven for 19–24 minutes, or until golden brown.
7. Cool on wire rack for 5 minutes before serving. Best served warm.

Chocolate, Cashew & Cherry Cookies
Makes 22 cookies

These tasty cookies make an almost instant dessert with ice cream or Greek yoghurt. Try dried apricots as a change from cranberries and cherries.

Preparation time: 10 mins
Cooking time: 15 mins

100g (4oz) softened polyunsaturated margarine or butter
100g (4oz) caster sugar
1 egg, size 3
150g (5oz) self-raising flour
10ml (2 teaspoons) cocoa powder

2.5ml (1/2 teaspoon) ground cinnamon
75g (3oz) dried cranberries and cherries or 75g (3oz) dried apricots, roughly chopped
75g (3oz) cashew nuts, roughly chopped

1. Pre-heat the oven to 375°F (190°C) gas mark 5.
2. Lightly grease two baking sheets.
3. Put all ingredients into a large mixing bowl and beat together to combine.
4. Put large teaspoonfuls of the mixture onto the baking sheets, leaving room to allow biscuits to spread a little. Flatten slightly with back of a damp fork.
5. Bake for 15 minutes, until golden and just firm to the touch.
6. Allow to cool on baking sheet for at least 10 minutes, then transfer to wire rack and leave to cool completely. Store in an airtight tin.

Hazelnut Biscuits

Serves 6 (makes approx. 24 biscuits)

Delicious with ice creams or sorbets, or just with a cup of tea. Keep the biscuits in an airtight tin. You may like to dip some of the biscuits in melted chocolate. Ground hazelnuts are available in supermarkets. They are considerably cheaper than ground almonds.

Preparation time: 10 mins
Cooking time: 14 mins

75g (3oz) butter, at room
  temperature
75g (3oz) caster sugar
Few drops vanilla essence

2 egg whites, size 3
50g (2oz) plain flour, sieved
50g (2oz) ground hazelnuts

To serve
sifted icing sugar

1. Pre-heat the oven to 400°F (200°C) gas mark 6. Grease two baking sheets.
2. In a large mixing bowl, cream together butter and sugar until soft and fluffy.
3. Beat in vanilla essence.
4. In a separate bowl, whisk egg whites until standing in soft peaks.
5. Quickly, using a wooden spoon, beat whisked egg whites into creamed mixture with 15ml (1 tablespoon) of the flour.
6. Fold in remaining flour with the ground hazelnuts.
7. Drop heaped teaspoonfuls of the mixture onto baking sheet, allowing room for biscuits to spread slightly.
8. Bake for 6–7 minutes or until just firm to the touch and pale golden round the edges.
9. Remove from baking sheet and cool on wire rack. Biscuits will harden as they cool. Serve dusted with a little sifted icing sugar.

Coffee Floater
Serves 6

Serve this ice cold coffee instead of a dessert on a warm summer's evening. Also popular at coffee or tea-time with some special biscuits.

Preparation time: 10 mins
Cooking time: 0

For the base

90ml (6 tablespoons) coffee essence
180ml (12 tablespoons) dark rum or coffee liqueur

1.5 litres (2¹/₂ pints) ice-cold semi-skimmed milk

For the topping

450ml (15 fl oz) double cream
75g (3oz) caster sugar

Sieved cocoa powder

1. In a mixing bowl, whip the cream until floppy and fold in the sugar.
2. In a large jug, blend the coffee essence with the rum and ice-cold milk.
3. Divide the coffee between six tumblers. Float cream topping evenly over coffees.
4. Serve immediately, sprinkled with a little sifted cocoa powder.

PART TWO

Introduction
to the Menu Section

Planning the menu for a special occasion can sometimes be more time-consuming and difficult than the entire rigmarole of shopping, preparing and final presentation of the meal. The task of leafing through endless cookbooks, selecting just enough well-balanced recipes to feed the right number of people and which complement each other in texture, colour and variety can seem endless.

The following menus have been carefully originated to enable you to entertain quickly and easily.

Designed with friends in mind, each menu presents imaginative, colourful and appealing spreads that don't rely too heavily on cordon bleu skills. Planned for various occasions, each menu is versatile and has been tried and tested in real entertaining circumstances, so enjoy glancing through the menus, to select one which would suit your next entertaining situation.

A few wine suggestions have been made, leaving you to plan your own drinks for the remainder.

Please note that timings on orders of menus are approximate. They also assume that you have all ingredients assembled and are ready to start. Treat them as a guide only.

Sunday Brunch

Serves 6

Brunch should be simple and friendly, giving guests the chance to enjoy each other's company, while sampling delicious home cooking. Orange juice and a well chilled sparkling wine are good served with brunch, with plenty of tea and fresh coffee, of course.

Menu

Fruity Gammon with Tomato Sauce
Easy Kedgeree
Anchovy & Tomato Baked Eggs (*see page 24*)
Sweetcorn with Herbs

~ ● ~

Greek Yoghurt with Fresh Fruits in Season
(clusters of seedless grapes, tangerines, strawberries, kiwi fruit, nectarines, small apples or chunks of fresh pineapple will be popular)

~ ● ~

Selection of bakery breads with butter, polyunsaturated margarine and low fat spreads, honey, jams and marmalade, or heat fresh croissants in the oven until crisp and serve with herby cream cheese or honey

~ ● ~

Pain au Chocolat (*see page 170*)

Order

1. About 1 hour before the meal, prepare the gammon and make the sauce.
2. Next, make the kedgeree and whilst it cooks, organise the table and prepare the eggs.
3. Finally, once your guests arrive, pop the eggs in to bake above the gammon.

4. Drain 2 × 340g (14oz) cans of sweetcorn and put in a bowl. Add 30ml (2 tablespoons) olive oil, a few drops of lemon juice and salt and pepper. Toss to coat, then serve sprinkled with a few snipped fresh herbs.
5. Turn the yoghurt into an attractive serving dish, top with a dessertspoon of demerara sugar and a shake of cinnamon.

Fruity Gammon with Tomato Sauce

Preparation time: 5 mins
Cooking time: 30 mins

6 gammon steaks, about 100g (4oz) each
Olive oil, for greasing
6 pineapple rings canned in natural juice, drained

30ml (6 teaspoons) pesto sauce
12 thin rashers streaky bacon, rinded

For the tomato sauce

1 × 400g (14oz) can chopped tomatoes with herbs

1 clove garlic, crushed
5ml (1 teaspoon) clear honey

To serve
salad garnish

1. Pre-heat the oven to 375°F (190°C) gas mark 5.
2. Arrange gammon in a lightly oiled roasting tin.
3. Top each steak with a pineapple ring and put 5ml (1 teaspoon) pesto in the centre of each ring.
4. Wrap 2 bacon rashers round each steak, leaving join underneath and forming a cross. Bake for 30 minutes.
5. Meanwhile, make the sauce. Place all ingredients in a food processor, process until smooth.
6. Turn into pan and heat, stirring continuously, until boiling.
7. Serve the gammon steaks on an attractive dish, garnished with salad. Offer the sauce separately in a warmed sauce boat.

Easy Kedgeree

This recipe is started on the hob, then completed in the microwave.

Preparation time: 15 mins
Cooking time: 17 mins

30ml (2 tablespoons) rape seed oil

2 medium red onions, peeled, sliced, then slices pushed into rings

250ml (8 fl oz) long grain rice, measured in a measuring jug

5ml (1 teaspoon) medium curry powder

600ml (1 pint) hot chicken stock

450g (1lb) finnan haddock fillet

30ml (2 tablespoons) milk

3 hard-boiled eggs, size 3, chopped

100g (4oz) peeled prawns, defrosted if frozen

30ml (2 tablespoons) freshly chopped parsley

1. Heat the oil in a large frying pan. Sauté the onions for about 12 minutes, until crisp and golden. Drain on absorbent kitchen paper. Set aside, but keep warm.
2. Meanwhile, put the rice into a large casserole dish. Add curry powder. Pour on the stock. Cover and microwave on 100%/FULL power for 9 minutes. Set aside, without removing the lid and allow to stand for 7 minutes.
3. Arrange haddock in a single layer on a plate. Pour over the milk. Cover and microwave on 100%/FULL power for 5–6 minutes, or until fish flakes easily.
4. Fork rice up, mixing in the flaked haddock (discard the milk, any bones and skin) with the eggs and prawns. Cover and return to microwave for 2 minutes on 100%/FULL power. Stir.
5. Serve immediately topped with the onion rings and sprinkled with parsley.

Lunch al Fresco

Serves 6

There is something magical about eating out of doors on a balmy summer's day. Set this meal out on a buffet table and allow guests to help themselves, then eat on the patio or in the garden. Try Semillon Chardonnay from southern Australia with this menu.

Menu

Marinated Haunch of Venison
Chicken Pâté
Smoked Salmon Parcels
Basket of mixed bread rolls and butter
Tomato, Olive & Basil Salad
Summer Salad

~ • ~

Watermelon Cream
Apple & Apricot Pâtisserie

Order

1. Prepare and cook the venison in advance and serve warm or cold.
2. About 1½ hours before the meal, prepare and bake the apple and apricot pâtisserie.
3. While the pastry bakes, prepare the chicken pâté and leave it in the fridge to chill.
4. Next, prepare the summer salad, then the tomato, olive and basil salad, but do not dress the summer salad until ready to serve. Chill until serving time.
5. 30 minutes before you want to eat, prepare the smoked salmon parcels, then the watermelon cream.
6. 10 minutes before, warm the rolls in the hot oven.

Marinated Haunch of Venison

Note: Venison is a delicious lean meat with a 'gamey' flavour. It should be served rare and is delicious warm or cold.

Preparation time: 10 mins + marinating time
Cooking time: 50-55 mins

25g (1oz) butter
10ml (2 teaspoons) olive oil

1 × 1kg (2lb) venison joint, rolled and tied ready for the oven, defrosted if necessary (now available frozen from supermarkets)

For the marinade

30ml (2 tablespoons) port
30ml (2 tablespoons) olive oil
Salt and freshly ground black pepper

15ml (1 tablespoon) freshly chopped herbs

To garnish
fresh sprigs of redcurrants

blanched mangetout

1. Pre-heat the oven to 425°F (220°C) gas mark 7.
2. Melt the butter with the 10ml (2 teaspoons) olive oil in a frying pan.
3. Blot the venison joint all over with absorbent kitchen paper, then brown venison on all sides in the pan. Remove pan from heat.
4. Mix together all ingredients for the marinade. Pour over venison and leave to marinate for 15 minutes (or overnight, if preferred).
5. Transfer to a roasting pan. Pour marinade over joint. Roast for 50-55 minutes, basting every 15 minutes or so.
6. Allow to stand for 15 minutes at least, before serving, garnished with the redcurrants and mangetout.

Chicken Pâté

Preparation time: 10 mins
Cooking time: 0

350g (12oz) chicken breast slice from the deli counter
225g (8oz) reduced fat cream cheese or cottage cheese
45ml (3 tablespoons) creamy fromage frais

10ml (2 teaspoons) tomato purée
30ml (2 tablespoons) fresh parsley sprigs
Freshly ground black pepper

To serve
warm crusty rolls or ciabatta bread

1. Coarsely chop the chicken.
2. If using cottage cheese, whizz it in the food processor until smooth, then add the chicken breast, fromage frais, tomato purée and parsley sprigs, then whizz again to blend.
3. If using cream cheese, put all ingredients except black pepper into food processor. Process to combine and until smooth, but still textured.
4. Season with a little black pepper.
5. Turn into a pâté dish and chill until ready to serve, or can be served immediately.

Smoked Salmon Parcels

Yummy, colourful parcels with an egg and cheese filling. They taste even better than they look.

Preparation time: 15 mins
Cooking time: 0

50g (2oz) le Roule soft cheese with herbs and garlic, at room temperature

50g (2oz) low fat soft cheese, at room temperature

45ml (3 tablespoons) mayonnaise	*4 eggs, size 3, hard-boiled and finely chopped*
10ml (2 teaspoons) lemon juice	*12 thin slices of smoked salmon*
Salt and freshly ground black pepper	*12 long chives*

To garnish
fresh coriander   *lemon wedges*

1. Prepare the filling. Put the cheeses into a mixing bowl. Add the mayonnaise and lemon juice and beat with a wooden spoon until smooth. Season to taste with a little salt and pepper, then fold in the egg.
2. Lay the smoked salmon slices out flat. Put a spoonful of mixture onto centre of each slice. Roll or fold into neat parcels. Tie each one with a chive.
3. Chill, covered, until ready to serve. Serve with the fresh coriander and wedges of lemon and any remaining filling.

Tomato, Olive & Basil Salad

Preparation time: 10 mins
Cooking time: 0

4 large Italian beef tomatoes   *100g (4oz) pitted black olives*

For the dressing

1 clove garlic, crushed	*15ml (1 tablespoon) fresh basil leaves, torn*
Juice of 1 lemon	
Grated rind of 1/2 lemon	*Salt and freshly ground black pepper*
45ml (3 tablespoons) virgin olive oil	

1. Slice the tomatoes thinly and arrange in a shallow dish. Add the olives.
2. Put all the ingredients for the dressing into a mug and whisk

with a fork. Pour dressing over salad. Cover and chill until ready to serve.

Summer Salad

Green salad with fruits and an olive oil dressing spiked with lemon is refreshing and colourful.

Preparation time: 10 mins
Cooking time: 0

1 Iceberg lettuce
1 bunch watercress, trimmed
¹/₂ cucumber, peeled and sliced

100g (4oz) strawberries, sliced
1 orange, segmented without
  pith or peel

For the dressing

90ml (6 tablespoons) virgin
  olive oil
30ml (2 tablespoons) lemon
  vinegar

15ml (1 tablespoon) freshly
  chopped parsley
Salt and freshly ground black
  pepper

1. Arrange the lettuce and watercress in a large salad bowl.
2. Add the cucumber, strawberries and orange.
3. Combine all ingredients for the dressing in a mug. Whisk to combine.
4. Pour dressing over salad. Toss to coat. Serve immediately.

Watermelon Cream

A light summery dessert that looks very pretty. Watermelon halves are readily available in supermarkets.

Preparation time: 10 mins
Cooking time: 0

*1/2 ripe watermelon, about
  1.5kg (3lb) in weight
225g (8oz) strawberries, hulled
  and sliced,* or *225g (8oz)
  seedless red grapes*

*50g (2oz) caster sugar
200g (7oz) Greek yoghurt
5ml (1 teaspoon) ground
  cinnamon*

1. Scoop out the flesh from the melon, using a dessertspoon.
   Reserve the skin. Roughly chop the flesh, discarding the
   black pips. Reserve any juice and serve in a jug beside the
   melon.
2. Put the melon flesh into a mixing bowl. Add the strawberries
   or grapes. Sprinkle sugar over.
3. Turn yoghurt into a clean mixing bowl.
4. Fold the fruit into the yoghurt with the ground cinnamon,
   reserving a few pieces for decoration.
5. Pile fruit and yoghurt back into melon shell. Decorate with
   remaining fruit and serve.

Apple & Apricot Pâtisserie

Preparation time: 15 mins
Cooking time: 20 mins

*1 × 450g (1lb) packet puff
  pastry, defrosted if frozen
1 × 350g (12oz) jar apple pie
  filling without sugar
8 ready-to-eat dried apricots,
  ⌐hopped up with scissors*

*Beaten egg, to glaze
25g (1oz) flaked almonds
15ml (1 tablespoon) caster
  sugar*

To serve
sifted icing sugar

fromage frais or *whipped
  whipping cream*

1. Pre-heat the oven to 425°F (220°C) gas mark 7.
2. Cut pastry into two equal halves. Roll pastry out to two
   rectangles, each measuring 25 × 33cm (10 × 13in). Put one
   rectangle onto a dampened baking sheet.

3. Blend together the apple pie filling and the apricots in a mixing bowl. Spoon onto centre of first piece of pastry, leaving a 1.25cm (½in) edge.

4. Moisten edge of pastry. Fold second rectangle of pastry in half, lengthways and make cuts 1.25cm (½in) apart to within 2cm (¾in) of the edge. Lift folded pastry onto apple mixture, then open out to fit over first piece exactly. Seal edges, knock up and flute edges.

5. Brush all over with beaten egg. Sprinkle with nuts and caster sugar.

6. Bake for 20 minutes, until golden. Serve warm, sprinkled with a snow of sifted icing sugar, accompanied by the fromage frais or whipping cream.

Italian Lunch

Serves 6

Italians love to serve a variety of dishes so that guests can help themselves to a little of each. A light sparkling wine such as Moscata Frizzante, well chilled, would be excellent with this meal.

Menu

Mascarpone Pasta
Chilled Spicy Pasta
Antipasta Platter
Italian Salad
Ciabatta (Italian flat bread) and Granary Rolls
~ ● ~
Italian Ice Cream with Fruit Sauce

Order

1. About 45 minutes before the meal, prepare the chilled spicy pasta. While the pasta is cooking, prepare and chill the fruit sauce, then complete the spicy pasta. Chill.
2. 20 minutes before the meal, prepare the Italian salad. Toss in dressing on serving.
3. Arrange the antipasta platter next and put it on the table as the centrepiece.
4. Lastly, about 10 minutes before you want to eat, prepare the mascarpone pasta and serve it steaming hot.

Mascarpone Pasta

Mascarpone is a full fat, soft, creamy Italian cheese, available in tubs from the chill counter of your supermarket. The creamy texture and wonderful flavour combines superbly with passata.

Preparation time: 10 mins
Cooking time: 8 mins

*450g (1lb) quick-cook dried
  spaghetti*
5ml (1 teaspoon) olive oil
500ml (17 fl oz) passata
Small bunch parsley sprigs

*5ml (1 teaspoon) hot chilli
  powder*
*150g (5oz) mascarpone cream
  cheese*
Salt

To serve
freshly chopped parsley

1. Cook the pasta in a large pan of boiling, salted water with the oil, according to directions (6–7 minutes). Stir once or twice during cooking to prevent pasta sticking.
2. Meanwhile, put the passata into the blender with the parsley, chilli powder and the cheese. Whizz to blend. Pour into a large pan and heat, stirring continuously until just simmering. Remove from heat and season to taste with the salt.
3. Turn the cooked, drained pasta into a large, warmed serving bowl.
4. Pour the tomato sauce over and toss to coat. Serve immediately, sprinkled with the chopped parsley.

Chilled Spicy Pasta

Preparation time: 10 mins
Cooking time: 12 mins

*350g (12oz) tri-colour dried
  pasta twists*
5ml (1 teaspoon) olive oil
*1 × 150ml (5 fl oz) carton
  Greek yoghurt*
150ml (5 fl oz) soured cream
1 clove garlic, crushed
5ml (1 teaspoon) curry powder
3 spring onions, chopped

*Salt and freshly ground black
  pepper*
*175g (6oz) frozen sweetcorn
  kernels, cooked and drained*
*1 × 411g (14.5oz) can cut
  asparagus spears, drained*
*400g (14oz) smoked trout or
  smoked mackerel, flaked*

To serve
Little Gem lettuce leaves

1. Cook the pasta in a large pan with plenty of boiling water and the oil, according to directions on the packet, until 'al dente' (10–12 minutes).
2. Meanwhile, make the dressing. In a large mixing bowl, blend the yoghurt and the soured cream. Stir in the garlic, curry powder and the spring onions. Season lightly with salt and pepper. Add the sweetcorn and asparagus, retaining a few asparagus tips for garnish.
3. Drain pasta and refresh under cold running water, then drain well and turn into the bowl with the dressing. Toss to coat. Turn into serving dish, edged with lettuce leaves.
4. Serve immediately, garnished with reserved asparagus tips and the smoked trout or mackerel.

Antipasta Platter

Antipasta is a perfect dish for entertaining as it can be prepared well in advance, then served to eat at leisure. The bite-sized morsels are arranged attractively on a large platter for guests to help themselves.

Preparation time: 10 mins
Cooking time: 0

225g (8oz) smoked Continental pork sausage, sliced
6 corchons (French gherkins)
1 × 50g (2oz) can anchovies with capers, drained
3 eggs, size 3, hard-boiled, shelled and halved

8 radishes, washed, trimmed and halved
75g (3oz) pitted black olives
100g (4oz) peppered salami, thinly sliced
1 × 125g (4½oz) pack Italian mozzarella cheese, drained and sliced

6 spring onions, trimmed
1 × 354g (12oz) can tuna
  chunks in oil, drained
1 × 400g (14oz) can artichoke
  hearts, drained and halved

6 sun-dried tomatoes in oil,
  well drained
2 Little Gem lettuces

To serve
coriander leaves or freshly chopped parsley

1. Arrange the ingredients attractively on a large meat plate.
2. Garnish with coriander leaves or freshly chopped parsley and
   serve immediately, or cover with cling film and chill in fridge
   until ready to serve.

Italian Salad

Preparation time: 10 mins
Cooking time: 0

1 head curly endive lettuce,
  well washed
1 small bunch watercress,
  brown leaves discarded
450g (1lb) Italian beef
  tomatoes, sliced

100g (4oz) pitted black olives
  (calamata, if possible),
  halved
30ml (2 tablespoons) freshly
  shredded basil leaves

For the dressing

60ml (4 tablespoons) olive oil
Juice of 1/2 lime

Salt and freshly ground black
  pepper

1. Shred the lettuce into a large bowl. Add the sprigs of
   watercress with the sliced tomatoes, halved olives and basil.
2. Sprinkle the olive oil and lime juice over the salad, season
   lightly with salt and pepper. Toss together to coat and serve
   immediately.

Italian Ice Cream with Fruit Sauce

Italian ice cream is readily available from leading supermarkets. Choose two varieties and serve scooped into sundae dishes, topped with the fruity sauce and decorated with special wafers.

To peel peaches, cover with boiling water. Stand for 1–2 minutes. Plunge into cold water, then skin will be easy to remove.

Preparation time: 15 mins + chilling time
Cooking time: 0

350g (12oz) raspberries, defrosted if frozen

2 large, ripe peaches, peeled, stoned and chopped

30ml (2 tablespoons) caster sugar

225g (8oz) strawberries, hulled and chopped

45ml (3 tablespoons) Crème de Cassis

1 litre (1³/₄ pints) vanilla Italian ice cream

1 litre (1³/₄ pints) tutti frutti Italian ice cream

To serve
crushed amaretti biscuits or wafers

1. Put the raspberries into a food processor with the peaches and caster sugar. Process to a purée. Pass through a sieve into a large mixing bowl.
2. Fold the strawberries and Crème de Cassis into the sauce. Cover and chill in the fridge for 10 minutes.
3. Serve a scoop of each variety of ice cream in sundae dishes with the fruit sauce spooned over, topped with crushed amaretti biscuits or decorated with wafers.

Almost Instant Lunch

Serves 6

Use convenience foods to produce an amazingly fast and fresh-tasting lunch for six. A bottle of chilled Chablis would go well with this menu.

Menu

Speedy Gazpacho
Fishy Pasta with two varieties of French bread
Continental Salad
~ • ~
Basket of fresh fruits in season
(choose contrasting colours, shapes and textures)
~ • ~
Piece of ripe Brie with oat biscuits and sesame crackers

Order

1. About 45 minutes before you want to serve the meal, prepare the gazpacho and chill in the fridge.
2. Leave the Brie to stand at room temperature.
3. Next, prepare the pasta dish.
4. While the pasta dish is in the oven, prepare the continental salad with its dressing, adding the dressing to the salad as you serve it. Lay out the fruit, either in a fruit bowl or on a large oval plate.
5. Heat the bread in the hot oven 10 minutes before serving, then slice and pile into a bread basket lined with a napkin.

Speedy Gazpacho

Note: If you prefer to make your own croûtons, simply cube day-old white and brown bread, crusts removed, and fry in a little olive oil, turning frequently, until golden. Drain on absorbent kitchen paper. It is important to serve the soup very cold.

Preparation time: 10 mins
Cooking time: 0

1 × 397g (14oz) can chopped tomatoes
1 × 7.5cm (3in) piece cucumber, peeled and chopped
1 small red pepper, seeded and chopped
2 spring onions, chopped
2 cloves garlic, chopped
30ml (2 tablespoons) parsley sprigs

45ml (3 tablespoons) olive oil
30ml (2 tablespoons) red wine vinegar
30ml (2 tablespoons) tomato purée
300ml (10 fl oz) vegetable juice
30ml (2 tablespoons) dry sherry
Salt and freshly ground black pepper

To serve
freshly chopped parsley   *croûtons*

1. Put the tomatoes, cucumber, red pepper, spring onions, garlic and parsley into the food processor.
2. Add the oil, vinegar and tomato purée. Process until smooth. Turn into a mixing bowl.
3. Stir in the vegetable juice and sherry. Season to taste with salt and pepper.
4. Cover and chill until ready to serve. If soup seems a little thick after chilling, stir in a little ice cold water.
5. Serve the soup with croûtons and freshly chopped parsley.

Fishy Pasta

Preparation time: 10 mins
Cooking time: 25 mins

275g (10oz) tri-colour dried
 pasta twists
5ml (1 teaspoon) sunflower oil
1 × 25g (1oz) packet
 hollandaise sauce mix
300ml (10 fl oz) milk
150ml (5 fl oz) whipping
 cream
1 × 411g (14oz) can cut
 asparagus spears, drained

1 × 200g (7oz) can tuna fish,
 drained and flaked
1 × 170g (5¼oz) can white
 crab meat
25g (1oz) Cheddar cheese,
 grated
50g (2oz) fresh brown
 breadcrumbs

1. Pre-heat the oven to 375°F (190°C) gas mark 5.
2. Cook the pasta in a large pan of boiling water with the oil, according to directions on the packet (10–12 minutes).
3. Meanwhile, combine the contents of the packet of hollandaise sauce with the milk in a large saucepan.
4. Bring to the boil, over a medium heat, stirring continuously. Allow to simmer, uncovered for 2–3 minutes. Remove from the heat.
5. Stir the cream into the sauce with the drained asparagus, flaked tuna fish, crab meat and the cooked pasta.
6. Heat over a gentle heat until thoroughly hot, stirring. Turn into a large, greased, ovenproof dish.
7. Sprinkle cheese and breadcrumbs over pie. Bake in the pre-heated oven for 15 minutes until crisp and golden. If topping has not browned to your liking, pop it under a pre-heated grill for a minute or two.

Continental Salad

Bags of prepared Continental salad leaves are readily available from supermarkets. They take the headache out of washing and spin-drying salad and often save money too, as you don't have to buy a host of different lettuces to obtain a few leaves of each. Several varieties now come with a separate pack of garlic croûtons enclosed.

Preparation time: 10 mins
Cooking time: 0

1 × 175–225g (6–8oz) bag ready-washed Continental salad leaves with garlic croûtons

100g (4oz) pitted black olives
225g (8oz) cherry tomatoes, halved
1 bunch spring onions, sliced

For the dressing

Juice of 1 lemon
90ml (6 tablespoons) olive oil
30ml (2 tablespoons) fresh
  basil leaves, torn

Salt and freshly ground black
  pepper

1. Turn the salad leaves into a salad bowl.
2. Toss in the olives with the tomatoes and onions.
3. Prepare the dressing. Put all ingredients into a mug and whisk with a fork.
4. Pour dressing over salad, toss to coat, then serve immediately, adding croûtons at the last minute.

Vegetarian Buffet

Serves 6

A tasty, varied feast for vegetarians and many others who prefer
not to over indulge in meat. Serve the meal buffet-style.

Menu

Pasta with Red Pesto & Parmesan
Cracked Wheat Surprise
Roasted Garlic Peppers
Dinner Party Mixed Salad (*see page 50*)
Assorted bread rolls with butter or vegetarian spread

~ ● ~

Syllabub (*see page 158*)
or
Fresh Fruit Platter

Order

1. Cook bulghar wheat and set aside about 45 minutes before you want to eat.
2. Prepare syllabub and chill or arrange fresh fruit on attractive oval dish.
3. Prepare dinner party salad, chill, adding dressing on serving. Pre-heat oven for peppers.
4. 20 minutes before the meal, boil peppers, drain and roast.
5. 15 minutes before the meal, cook pasta and complete cracked wheat surprise. Warm the bread rolls in the oven.
6. Serve salad, adding dressing. Serve cracked wheat surprise, adding nuts. Serve peppers.
7. Drain pasta, add pesto sauce, oil and seasoning. Toss, then serve.

Pasta with Red Pesto & Parmesan

Preparation time: 5 mins
Cooking time: 14 mins

450g (1lb) fusilli dried pasta twists
Olive oil
1 × 190g (6¹/₂oz) jar red pesto sauce

Salt and freshly ground black pepper
Grated Parmesan cheese

1. Cook the pasta in a large saucepan with plenty of boiling water and 5ml (1 teaspoon) olive oil, for 9–11 minutes, until 'al dente' (to the tooth). Stir occasionally during cooking to prevent sticking.
2. Drain pasta and return to pan. Add pesto sauce to pan, stirring to coat.
3. Stir in enough olive oil to form a smooth sauce. Season to taste with a little salt and pepper. Re-heat gently, stirring.
4. Turn into a warmed serving dish and serve sprinkled with the grated Parmesan.

Cracked Wheat Surprise

Note: The warm bulghur wheat quickly takes on the flavours of the other ingredients.

Preparation time: 10 mins
Cooking time: 5 mins + standing time

350g (12oz) bulghur wheat
2 sticks celery, chopped
3 eggs, size 2, hard-boiled and chopped
1 × 400g (14oz) can chopped tomatoes
30ml (2 tablespoons) olive oil
15ml (1 tablespoon) freshly chopped parsley

100g (4oz) pimento stuffed olives, halved
15ml (1 tablespoon) soy sauce
1 × 430g (15oz) can red kidney beans, drained
75g (3oz) stoned dates, chopped
Salt and freshly ground black pepper

To serve
bed of lettuce
50g (2oz) chopped walnuts

grated Parmesan cheese

1. Put the bulghur wheat into a large pan. Cover with 1.5 litres (2½ pints) boiling water and simmer, covered with a lid, for 5 minutes. Remove from heat and set aside for 15 minutes, covered.
2. Meanwhile, in a large mixing bowl, combine the celery with the eggs, tomatoes, oil, parsley and olives. Add the soy sauce and red kidney beans with the dates. Toss together.
3. Drain the bulghur wheat through a sieve and add to the bowl. Season lightly and toss everything together to mix well.
4. Arrange the shredded lettuce on a large serving dish and turn the bulghur mixture into the centre.
5. Serve sprinkled with the chopped walnuts and the Parmesan.

Roasted Garlic Peppers

Pretty peppers, quickly oven-roasted, taste simply wonderful.

Preparation time: 10 mins
Cooking time: 19 mins

2 small red peppers
2 small green peppers
2 small yellow peppers
2 small orange peppers
2 cloves garlic, crushed

About 30ml (2 tablespoons)
* olive oil*
Salt and freshly ground black
* pepper*
10ml (2 teaspoons) sesame
* seeds*

1. Pre-heat the oven to 400°F (200°C) gas mark 6.
2. Halve and seed the peppers, then cut each half in two lengthways. Meanwhile, bring a pan of water to the boil.
3. Add peppers, cover and simmer for 4 minutes.
4. Meanwhile, lightly oil roasting tin.
5. Drain peppers and turn into prepared tin.
6. Stir crushed garlic into the oil, then brush evenly over both sides of peppers. Season with a little salt and pepper. Sprinkle insides of the peppers with sesame seeds.
7. Bake for 15–20 minutes, until tinged brown.

Vegetarian Feast

Serves 6

This quick colourful spread is tasty and filling. The dessert is good served warm or cold.

Menu

Mexican Dip
~ • ~
Cheese & Vegetable Flan
Spiced Mushroom Bean Feast
Crunchy Winter Salad (*see page 228*)
Fresh bread rolls
~ • ~
Honey, Apricots & Prunes with Greek Yoghurt
or fromage frais

Order

1. About 1 hour before you want to serve the meal, pre-heat the oven for the flan. Prepare the dessert – use microwave method, if possible. Prepare and cook the flan.
2. Prepare the crunchy winter salad next and chill.
3. Prepare the bean feast and leave it simmering. Pop the bread in the oven to warm.
4. 15 minutes before the meal, prepare the Mexican dip and crudités. Serve.
5. Serve the salad, adding the dressing. Serve the spiced mushroom bean feast.

Mexican Dip

Mexican food is popular with almost everyone. Try this light dip with vegetable crudités and tortilla chips for an interesting starter. Try to find the rough skinned, almost black avocados for their excellent flavour.

Preparation time: 10 mins
Cooking time: 0

3 large, ripe avocados
Juice of 1 fresh lime
2 cloves garlic, crushed
Dash of chilli sauce
60ml (4 tablespoons) fromage
  frais

45ml (3 tablespoons) freshly
  chopped parsley
Salt and freshly ground black
  pepper

To serve
vegetable sticks   *tortilla chips*

1. Halve avocados and remove stones. Scoop out the flesh and mash it in a mixing bowl.
2. Add lime juice, garlic, chilli sauce, fromage frais and parsley. Mix well. Season to taste, adding more chilli sauce if you like it hot!
3. Serve immediately or allow to stand, covered, for up to 45 minutes.

Cheese & Vegetable Flan

Preparation time: 15 mins
Cooking time: 20 mins

For the flan case

150g (5oz) filo pastry,
  defrosted (you will need 6
  sheets of filo)

Approx. 60ml (4 tablespoons)
  olive oil

For the filling

1 onion, finely chopped
2 sticks celery, finely chopped

450g (1lb) courgettes, chopped
100g (4oz) mushrooms, sliced

5ml (1 teaspoon) dried
   oregano
Salt and freshly ground black
   pepper

175g (6oz) vegetarian Cheddar
   cheese, grated
2.5ml (1/2 teaspoon) paprika

1. Pre-heat the oven to 400°F (200°C) gas mark 6.
2. Line the base and sides of a 20cm (8in) plain flan or sandwich tin with oiled sheets of filo pastry. Leave the pastry edges overlapping the tin.
3. Place on a baking sheet and bake for 5–8 minutes, or until golden.
4. Heat remaining oil in a large frying pan, then fry the onion and celery for 5 minutes, until softened.
5. Add courgettes, mushrooms and oregano and cook over a gentle heat, covered, for about 10 minutes, until the vegetables soften. Stir occasionally. Season to taste.
6. Put half the vegetables into the flan. Cover with half the grated cheese. Top with remaining vegetables, then sprinkle on the rest of the cheese. Sprinkle with the paprika.
7. Reduce oven temperature to 375°F (190°C) gas mark 5 and return flan to oven for about 10 minutes, until cheese melts and starts to brown. Best served warm.

Spiced Mushroom Bean Feast

A spicy vegetable dish that's useful for so many occasions. Popular with non-vegetarians, too. You may like to serve a bowl of creamy fromage frais, topped with a dusting of paprika, and warm bread rolls to accompany.

Preparation time: 15 mins
Cooking time: 26 mins

15ml (1 tablespoon) sunflower
   oil
1 large onion, chopped
2 sticks celery, chopped
2 cloves garlic, crushed

350g (12oz) chestnut
   mushrooms, sliced
30ml (2 tablespoons) tomato
   purée
5ml (1 teaspoon) paprika

1.25ml (¹/₄ teaspoon) dried
   crushed chillies
5ml (1 teaspoon) dried
   oregano
10ml (2 teaspoons) Marmite or
   other yeast extract spread

1 × 400g (14oz) can chopped
   tomatoes
2 × 430g (15oz) cans red
   kidney beans with their
   liquid
50g (2oz) sultanas
10ml (2 teaspoons) cornflour

1. Heat the oil in a large flameproof casserole dish.
2. Add onion, celery and garlic and sauté for 5 minutes.
3. Add the mushrooms, tomato purée, paprika, chillies, oregano, yeast extract, chopped tomatoes, red kidney beans with their liquid and the sultanas.
4. Stir well, then bring to the boil and simmer for 20 minutes.
5. Blend cornflour to a smooth paste with 30ml (2 tablespoons) water and stir into the pan. Continue to cook, stirring for a further minute, until slightly thickened. Serve immediately.

Honey, Apricots & Prunes

Preparation time: 5 mins
Cooking time: 12 mins by microwave or 25 mins conventional

250g (9oz) ready-to-use dried
   apricots
6 large, ready-to-eat agen
   prunes
Juice of ¹/₂ lemon

150ml (5 fl oz) Sauternes or
   medium sweet white wine
30ml (2 tablespoons) runny
   honey
2.5cm (1in) piece of cinnamon
   stick

To serve
25g (1oz) honey-roasted
   sunflower seeds

Greek yoghurt

1. If using a microwave, put the apricots and the prunes into a 1.2 litre (2 pint) microwavable bowl. Add the lemon juice and the wine. Pour over 300ml (10 fl oz) boiling water and stir in the honey. Add the cinnamon stick.
2. Cover and microwave on 100%/FULL power for 12 minutes. Set aside, covered, for at least 15 minutes, or until ready to serve.
3. For conventional cooks, put the apricots and prunes into a large saucepan. Add remaining ingredients. Simmer, covered, for 25 minutes. (These can be left simmering whilst you eat the first two courses.)
4. Remove the cinnamon stick and serve the fruits, warm or cold, topped with the sunflower seeds and accompanied by the Greek yoghurt.

A Chinese Dinner

Serves 4

Guests should help themselves to a little of each of these dishes which are all served at the same time. Make sure the dinner plates are piping hot when you serve the food.

Serve with ice cold lager, or try a chilled Sicilian white wine.

Menu

Peppered Chicken Stir-fry
Special Fried Rice
Easy Peasy Curry Sauce (*see page 126*)
Lamb Satay
Glazed Baby Sweetcorn

~ ● ~

Fresh Pineapple & Melon, prepared between courses

Order

1. Make the curry sauce well in advance and re-heat to serve.
2. About 1 hour before the meal, cook the rice and, while it is boiling, prepare the lamb and leave in the marinade mixture.
3. Next, prepare and cook the peppered chicken stir-fry and the glazed baby sweetcorn. Both dishes may be re-heated briefly when ready to serve.
4. Now prepare the lamb for grilling, then complete the special fried rice.
5. As you complete the fried rice dish, re-heat the peppered chicken and the sweetcorn gently, until thoroughly hot. Finally, grill the lamb.

Peppered Chicken Stir-fry

Preparation time: 15 mins
Cooking time: 8 mins

*1 yellow, 1 red and 1 green
pepper, seeded
2 medium carrots, peeled
45ml (3 tablespoons) olive oil*

*450g (1lb) chicken breast fillet,
cut into strips
175g (6oz) thin green beans
175g (6oz) button mushrooms,
sliced*

1. Cut the peppers and the carrots into matchsticks.
2. Heat the oil in a wok. Stir-fry the chicken for 3–4 minutes, until golden.
3. Add the remaining ingredients and stir-fry for a further 4–5 minutes. Serve immediately.

Special Fried Rice

Home-made special fried rice is particularly tasty, yet quick and easy to make. Serve any leftovers the next day as a rice salad. Measure the rice and water in the same measuring jug.

Preparation time: 10 mins
Cooking time: 20–24 mins if using white rice, 40 mins if using brown rice

*350ml (12 fl oz) long grain
white rice or brown rice
720ml (24 fl oz) chicken stock
30ml (2 tablespoons) sunflower
oil
1 large carrot, cut into
matchsticks
1 small red pepper, seeded and
diced*

*10ml (2 teaspoons) five-spice
powder
1 clove garlic, crushed
1 bunch spring onions,
chopped on the diagonal
100g (4oz) fresh bean sprouts,
well washed and drained
45ml (3 tablespoons) light soy
sauce*

175g (6oz) cooked prawns,
   defrosted if frozen

175g (6oz) cooked chicken
   breast, diced

1. Put the rice into a large pan with the stock. Bring to the boil,
   then cover and simmer for approx. 15 minutes for white rice
   or 35 minutes for brown rice, until rice is cooked and water
   has been more or less absorbed. Remove pan from heat and
   set aside, covered, but drain rice if necessary first.
2. Heat the oil in a wok or large frying pan.
3. Add the carrots with the red pepper. Stir-fry for 3 minutes.
   Add the five-spice powder with the garlic and continue to
   stir-fry for 1–2 minutes.
4. Add the spring onions and bean sprouts. Stir-fry for 2
   minutes. Add soy sauce, prawns and the chicken breast with
   the rice. Stir-fry for 4 minutes, until everything is thoroughly
   hot. Serve immediately.

Lamb Satay

This marinated lamb cooks so quickly and is a deliciously
different Chinese dish. Soak the bamboo skewers in water for at
least 15 minutes to prevent them burning.
   Note: For a change, use skinned chicken breast fillet instead of
the lamb.

Preparation time: 15 mins + marinating time
Cooking time: 4–6 mins

1kg (2lb) lean leg of lamb fillet,
   cut into 2.5cm (1in) cubes

For the marinade

75ml (5 tablespoons) dry white
   wine
45ml (3 tablespoons) peanut
   butter

30ml (2 tablespoons) soy sauce
30ml (2 tablespoons) yellow
   bean sauce
1 clove garlic, crushed

*1.25ml (¹/₄ teaspoon) hot chilli
    powder*

1. Put the lamb into a large mixing bowl.
2. Blend all the ingredients for the marinade and pour over the lamb. Set aside for 15 minutes at room temperature or cover and chill overnight.
3. Skewer the lamb and cook under a pre-heated hot grill for 2–3 minutes each side. Serve immediately.

Glazed Baby Sweetcorn

Note: Clarified butter is available from the chill compartment of large supermarkets.

Preparation time: 5 mins
Cooking time: 6 mins

*75g (3oz) clarified butter
30ml (2 tablespoons) dark soy
    sauce
2.5ml (¹/₂ teaspoon) five-spice
    powder*

*1 clove garlic, crushed
450g (1lb) frozen baby
    sweetcorn*

1. Put the butter into a large frying pan with the soy sauce, five-spice powder and the garlic. Heat gently, until melted and foamy.
2. Add the sweetcorn and stir-fry for about 5 minutes, until tender and crisp. Serve immediately.

A Family Occasion

Serves 6

This popular spicy chilli with garlic bread transforms a family get-together into an occasion. Serve the chilli straight from the pan with a soup ladle – it's quick and easy and you're less likely to spill any! The frozen dessert will keep for up to 3 months in the freezer, so make it well in advance. It's great as a standby for lots of occasions. Serve with well chilled lager and mineral water.

Menu

Spicy Chilli with Parsley Rice
Special Green Salad (*see page 53*)
Speedy Garlic & Parsley Bread
~ ● ~
Freezer Fruity Pud
or
Fresh Strawberry Dippers (*see page 153*)

Order

1. Prepare the freezer fruity pud well in advance.
2. 40 minutes before the meal, prepare the chilli; leave simmering. Prepare strawberry dippers.
3. 30 minutes before the meal, transfer the freezer fruity pud from the freezer to the fridge, turning it onto the serving dish and adding the decoration on serving.
4. Next, make the salad and chill in the fridge but add the dressing at the last minute.
5. Pre-heat the oven for the garlic bread.
6. Prepare a large pan of boiled rice. On serving, fork approx. 45ml (3 tablespoons) freshly chopped parsley into the rice.
7. Whilst the rice is cooking, prepare and cook the garlic bread.

Spicy Chilli

Preparation time: 5 mins
Cooking time: 40 mins

30ml (2 tablespoons) olive oil
2 medium onions, chopped
2 rashers streaky bacon, rinded and chopped
2 cloves garlic, crushed or finely chopped
750g (1½lb) lean minced beef
15ml (1 tablespoon) plain flour
2 × 400g (14oz) cans plum tomatoes

1 wine glass red wine
30ml (2 tablespoons) tomato purée
1 beef stock cube, crumbled
5ml (1 teaspoon) crushed dried chillies or 10ml (2 teaspoons) chilli powder
1 large green pepper, seeded and chopped
2 × 430g (15oz) cans red kidney beans, drained

To serve
freshly chopped parsley

boiled rice

1. Heat the oil in a large, flameproof casserole. Sauté the onions, bacon and garlic for 5 minutes.
2. Turn the heat up a little, add the beef and brown it, stirring now and again – this takes about 7 minutes.
3. Stir in the flour, then add the tomatoes with any juice, the red wine, tomato purée, stock cube, chilli, green pepper and red kidney beans. Stir well, breaking up the tomatoes. Cover and simmer for 30 minutes.
4. Serve the chilli sprinkled with the chopped parsley, accompanied by a bowl of steaming boiled rice and perhaps garlic bread (see below).

Speedy Garlic & Parsley Bread

Preparation time: 5 mins
Cooking time: 15 mins

75g (3oz) softened butter
2 cloves garlic, crushed
5ml (1 teaspoon) dried parsley

Freshly ground black pepper
1 French stick

1. Pre-heat the oven to 400°F (200°C) gas mark 6.
2. Put the butter into a mixing bowl. Add the garlic and the parsley. Season lightly with black pepper. Beat together with a wooden spoon, until combined.
3. Cut the loaf into 4cm (1½in) slices.
4. Spread each slice evenly and liberally on one side with the prepared butter. Arrange on baking sheets, butter side up.
5. Bake towards the top of the oven for 10–15 minutes, until crisp and golden. Serve immediately.

Freezer Fruity Pud

You will need a 1kg (2lb) loaf tin, lightly oiled and lined with baking parchment or foil.

Preparation time: 20 mins
Cooking time: 0

75g (3oz) polyunsaturated margarine or butter
225g (8oz) chocolate digestive biscuits, crushed
1 lemon jelly tablet

Grated rind and juice of 2 lemons
3 eggs, size 2, separated
75g (3oz) caster sugar
1 × 284ml (9 fl oz) carton whipping cream, whipped

To decorate
fresh raspberries or strawberries, sliced

1. Melt the margarine or butter in a medium-sized saucepan. Stir in the crushed biscuits.
2. Pour half the mixture into the prepared tin. Press down firmly. Freeze.
3. Dissolve the jelly in 150ml (5 fl oz) boiling water. Set aside.

Allow to cool. Strain the lemon juice and stir into the jelly with the rind.

4. Whisk the egg yolks with the caster sugar until thick. (This will take about 10 minutes with an electric whisk.)

5. Fork the whipped cream into the whisked mixture, using a metal spoon, then fold in the jelly mixture.

6. In a clean bowl, whisk the egg whites until stiff, then fold in.

7. Pour into loaf tin and sprinkle remaining chocolate crumbs over the top.

8. Freeze for at least 3 hours, or can be kept frozen for up to 3 months.

9. To serve, transfer to refrigerator for 30 minutes, then turn out onto serving dish and decorate with the fresh fruit. Serve in thin slices.

A Dinner to Impress

Serves 4

This dinner party is very easy to prepare and cook – and will impress even your boss! The sauce for the duck can be prepared in advance and re-heated while you quickly cook the duck, just before serving the starter. Leave the cooked duck in the warm pan while eating the starter – the texture will improve on standing and as long as you serve the sauce red hot, the meat will not seem cold. Fresh Fruit Brûlée makes a sensational dessert. Serve a well chilled Californian Chablis with the salmon and a good French white wine, such as Pouilly Fumé or a red St. Emilion, with the duck.

As presentation is all important, leave yourself time to decorate and garnish the food as described.

Menu

Potted Trout with Mangetout

~ ● ~

Fanned Duckling with Whisky Sauce & Kumquats (*see page 92*)
Microwave Medley of Fresh Vegetables

~ ● ~

Fresh Fruit Brûlée (*see page 144*)

Order

1. Earlier in the day, make the potted trout and chill in the fridge until ready to serve. (Can be made day before.)
2. About 50 minutes before you want to eat, prepare the fresh fruit brûlée. Chill in the fridge but have the sugar weighed out ready to sprinkle over.
3. 40 minutes before the meal, prepare the vegetables and put them ready to cook in the microwave when you are eating the first course.
4. Cook the sauce for the duck and leave it to be re-heated.
5. Cook the duck and the vegetables.
6. Cook the mangetout, garnish the starters and serve.
7. Re-heat the sauce between courses.
8. Brown the fresh fruit brûlée between courses.

Potted Trout with Mangetout

Potted fresh trout has a delicate flavour which is complemented by the fresh dill. Serve well chilled with crisp brown bread rolls. For a change, try fresh salmon in this recipe, instead of trout.

Preparation time: 5 mins
Cooking time: 5 mins

225g (8oz) fresh rainbow trout fillets
150ml (5 fl oz) milk

100g (4oz) butter
15ml (1 tablespoon) mayonnaise

5ml (1 teaspoon) lemon juice
15ml (1 tablespoon) freshly
chopped dill

Salt and freshly ground black
pepper

To serve
175g (6oz) mangetout
(optional)

wedges of lemon

1. Put the trout into a frying pan with the milk. Cover with a lid and poach until just cooked (3 minutes).
2. Flake into food processor, discarding skin.
3. Melt the butter in a small pan, over a low heat and when *just* melted, pour into food processor. Add mayonnaise, lemon juice and dill. Process just to blend. Season to taste.
4. Fill individual ramekins or similar small dishes with the mixture and chill in fridge until set (at least 40 minutes).
5. When ready to serve, simmer the mangetout in a little water for 3 minutes, until tender crisp. Drain and rinse with cold water.
6. Serve the ramekins on medium-sized plates with a garnish of mangetout, accompanied by wedges of lemon.

Microwave Medley of Fresh Vegetables

Vegetables cooked in the microwave taste fresh and full of flavour. They keep their bright colour, too. Stir once for even cooking – see method.

Preparation time: 10 mins
Cooking time: 11 mins + standing time

225g (8oz) courgettes, sliced at
an angle
225g (8oz) carrots, cut into
matchsticks
1 small red pepper, seeded and
roughly chopped

12 tiny new potatoes, scrubbed
clean and pricked once
30ml (2 tablespoons) white
wine (optional)

To serve
knob of butter   *freshly chopped parsley*

1. Put all the prepared vegetables into a large casserole or bowl.
2. Add 30ml (2 tablespoons) water or white wine if you have a bottle open.
3. Cover and microwave on 100%/FULL power for 11 minutes, stirring once after 5 minutes. Allow to stand, covered, for 3–4 minutes, then add the knob of butter and sprinkle with parsley as you serve.

Microwave Magic

Serves 4

A quick, easy and colourful two-course dinner party menu to serve four which is cooked in the microwave oven.

Menu

Trout with Almonds
Rice with Red Pepper & Corn
Dressed Little Gems
~ ● ~
Chocolate Orange Pots (*see page 157*)

Order

1. Prepare the chocolate orange pots at least 1 hour before you want to serve the first course. Chill in fridge until ready to serve.
2. About 20 minutes before the meal, prepare and cook the rice dish. Set aside, covered, on the worktop.
3. Cook the trout and toast the almonds under the grill while the fish is in the microwave.
4. Prepare the Little Gems – simply toss the washed, drained leaves in a vinaigrette (try the one on page 37) and serve it in a salad bowl.
5. Fork up rice to serve. Scatter almonds over fish and serve.

Trout with Almonds

Preparation time: 10 mins
Cooking time: 9^1/$_2$ mins

4 rainbow trout, each approx.
225g (8oz), cleaned and
gutted
50g (2oz) butter
1 clove garlic, crushed

Salt and freshly ground black
pepper
50g (2oz) flaked almonds
250ml (8 fl oz) soured cream

To garnish
sprigs of fresh parsley

1. Use a small piece of foil to wrap the tails of each fish to prevent them over-cooking.
2. Make two small incisions in the side of each fish with a sharp knife.
3. Put the butter into a suitable serving dish that will hold the fish in a single layer.
4. Microwave the butter in the serving dish for about 1½ minutes on 100%/FULL power, or until melted.
5. Stir the garlic into the melted butter and season lightly.
6. Arrange the fish, nose to tail in the flavoured butter.
7. Cover with cling film and microwave on 100%/FULL power for 8 minutes. Turn each fish over once halfway through cooking. Set aside, covering the dish with foil.
8. Toast the almonds under a pre-heated grill, until golden.
9. Pour the cream over the fish and microwave on power 4 or simmer for 5 minutes.
10. Serve immediately, sprinkled with the toasted nuts and garnished with parsley.

Rice with Red Pepper & Corn

Preparation time: 10 mins
Cooking time: 20 mins

300ml (10 fl oz) long grain
rice, measured in a
measuring jug
5ml (1 teaspoon) olive oil
100g (4oz) frozen sweetcorn

½ red pepper, seeded and
chopped
30ml (2 tablespoons) freshly
chopped parsley

1. Put rice, 650ml (22 fl oz) boiling water and oil into 2.25 litre (4 pint) mixing bowl. Cover.
2. Microwave on 100%/FULL power for 10 minutes. Set aside, covered, for 10 minutes.
3. Meanwhile, put sweetcorn and red pepper into a small bowl. Add 30ml (2 tablespoons) water. Cover and microwave on 100%/FULL power for 5 minutes.
4. Fork the sweetcorn and peppers into the rice, after its standing time, with the parsley. Turn into a warmed serving dish and serve immediately.

Supper on a Shoe String

Serves 6

A delicious supper menu for six that certainly won't break the bank.

Menu

Fettuccine with Pink Salmon & Asparagus
Speedy Salad
Ready Prepared Frozen Garlic Bread (from the supermarket)
~ ● ~
Microwave Marmalade Cake with Greek Yoghurt
or
Lemon Snow (*see page 152*)

Order

1. Prepare the marmalade cake first, about 1 hour before you want to eat, so that it has time to cool.

2. About 30 minutes before the meal, prepare the salad. Cover and chill until ready to serve.
3. Pre-heat the oven for the garlic bread according to instructions on packet.
4. 15 minutes before you want to eat, prepare and cook the sauce for the pasta. Pop the bread in the oven.
5. Cook the pasta and while it cooks, make dressing and toss salad. Serve salad. Place cake on serving plate and put yoghurt into bowl beside it. Sprinkle with a little ground cinnamon or ginger, if liked.
6. Drain pasta and serve, topped with the sauce.

Fettuccine with Pink Salmon & Asparagus

Preparation time: 5 mins
Cooking time: 15 mins

25g (1oz) butter
1 medium onion, chopped
1 clove garlic, crushed
15ml (1 tablespoon) tomato purée
300ml (10 fl oz) chicken stock
Salt and freshly ground black pepper
450g (1lb) fettuccine verdi

5ml (1 teaspoon) olive oil
300ml (10 fl oz) single cream
10ml (2 teaspoons) cornflour
1 × 418g (15oz) can pink salmon, drained and flaked, discarding skin and bones
1 × 411g (14¹/₂oz) can cut asparagus spears, drained

To serve
freshly chopped parsley

1. Melt the butter in a large frying pan. Sauté the onion and garlic for 4–5 minutes, until softened.
2. Add tomato purée, chicken stock and seasoning. Stir and bring to boiling point. Boil for about 4 minutes, or until reduced by half. Remove from heat.
3. Meanwhile, cook the pasta in a large pan of boiling water with the oil, according to directions on the packet (10–12 minutes).

4. Add cream to the onion mixture. Blend cornflour with 15ml (1 tablespoon) water and add to the pan. Bring slowly to simmering point, stirring, then simmer for 1–2 minutes. Add salmon and asparagus and re-heat gently.
5. Drain pasta and return to pan. Add the hot sauce. Toss together lightly and serve immediately on warmed dinner plates, sprinkled with the chopped parsley.

Speedy Salad

Shred the cabbage and grate the carrots in the food processor. A sprig of chopped celery leaves will add flavour to this slaw.

Preparation time: 10 mins
Cooking time: 0

225g (8oz) red cabbage, shredded
1/2 head celery, finely chopped
3 medium carrots, grated
150ml (5 fl oz) natural yoghurt
5ml (1 teaspoon) tomato purée
5ml (1 teaspoon) granary mustard
A few drops lemon juice
Salt and freshly ground black pepper
Grated rind and juice of 1/2 orange
25g (1oz) packet honey-roasted sunflower seeds

1. Put the shredded cabbage into a salad bowl. Add the celery and the grated carrot.
2. Put the yoghurt into a small bowl. Add the tomato purée and the mustard with the lemon juice. Blend until smooth. Season to taste with salt and pepper.
3. Pour the dressing over the salad. Add orange rind and juice. Toss to coat, then serve sprinkled with the sunflower seeds.

Microwave Marmalade Cake

Preparation time: 10 mins
Cooking time: 8–10 mins

150ml (5 fl oz) sunflower oil
100g (4oz) soft dark brown
  sugar
3 eggs, size 3
45ml (3 tablespoons) coarse
  cut marmalade
175g (6oz) wholemeal
  self-raising flour

5ml (1 teaspoon) baking
  powder
5ml (1 teaspoon) cinnamon
Rind and juice of 1 small
  orange
50g (2oz) chopped walnuts

To serve
sifted icing sugar   Greek yoghurt (optional)

1. Lightly grease and base line with non-stick baking parchment either a 22cm (9in) microwave ring mould, or a 1.75 litre (3 pint) microwave loaf pan.
2. Put all ingredients, except for the walnuts, into a large mixing bowl.
3. Using a wooden spoon, beat to form a smooth batter, then continue to beat for 1 minute. Stir in the walnuts. Turn into container.
4. Microwave on 100%/FULL power for 8–10 minutes, until a wooden cocktail stick inserted in the centre comes out clean. Leave to stand for 10 minutes.
5. Turn out onto a wire rack and allow to cool.
6. Serve, sprinkled with the icing sugar and accompanied by the yoghurt, if using.

Impromptu Supper

Serves 6

An easy, yet delicious two-course meal that's suitable for an after-theatre supper or for an impromptu lunch. Try a bottle or two of Chianti with this meal.

Menu

Almost Instant Pasta Supper
Crunchy Winter Salad
Crusty Bread Rolls and Butter
~ ● ~
Sherry Banana Splits (*see page 149*)

Order

1. About 30 minutes before you want to eat, cook the pasta and whilst it cooks, make the sauce and slice the ham for the pasta dish.
2. 20 minutes before the meal, prepare the bread in a basket lined with a napkin.
3. By now the pasta should be cooked, so complete the pasta dish and pop it under the grill.
4. Keep one eye on the pasta, but get the bananas and the bowls, etc., ready for the dessert. Prepare the desserts between courses.
5. Prepare and serve the crunchy winter salad.

Almost Instant Pasta Supper

A very simple dish that tastes sensational. Packet soup makes a good instant sauce for pasta.

Preparation time: 10 mins
Cooking time: 15 mins

1 × 500g (17¹/₂oz) packet dried fusilli pasta twists
5ml (1 teaspoon) corn oil
1 × 65g (2¹/₂oz) packet cream of chicken, no simmer, 1-pint soup
10ml (2 teaspoons) wholegrain mustard
1 × 397g (14oz) can chopped tomatoes
1 × 200g (7oz) can creamed mushrooms

30ml (2 tablespoons) freshly chopped basil
1 × 340g (12oz) can sweetcorn and peppers, drained
175g (6oz) smoked ham, cut into thin strips, or 175g (6oz) cooked chicken, cubed
100g (4oz) stoned black olives, halved
Freshly ground black pepper
Butter, for greasing

For the topping

50g (2oz) fresh brown breadcrumbs
50g (2oz) Cheddar cheese, crumbled

15ml (1 tablespoon) grated Parmesan cheese

To garnish
fresh basil leaves

1. Cook the fusilli, with the oil, in a large pan of boiling water for 9–11 minutes until 'al dente'. Stir once or twice during cooking to prevent pasta sticking. Pre-heat grill to medium hot.
2. Meanwhile make up soup in a large pan exactly according to directions on packet, adding the mustard with the water.
3. Add tomatoes, mushrooms, basil, sweetcorn, ham or chicken and olives to soup. Season with freshly ground black pepper. Stir well, then heat, stirring, until simmering.

4. Drain pasta and return to pan. Pour soup mixture over. Toss to coat. Turn into a large, lightly greased dish.
5. Combine breadcrumbs and cheeses and sprinkle over pasta evenly.
6. Pop under the pre-heated grill until crisp and golden. Serve immediately garnished with the basil.

Crunchy Winter Salad

This salad has plenty of crunchy texture and is ideal either on a buffet table or served with a hot casserole or stew. Prepare 2–3 hours in advance or at the last minute, according to your schedule. Use a food processor to shred fennel and cabbage if available.

Note: The avocado must be added to the salad on serving, otherwise it will discolour.

Preparation time: 10 mins
Cooking time: 0

1 head fennel, finely sliced
225g (8oz) red cabbage, finely shredded
175g (6oz) seedless white grapes

1 medium-sized ripe avocado pear
50g (2oz) toasted pine nuts or chopped pecan nuts
Grated rind and juice of $1/2$ lemon

75ml (5 tablespoons) olive oil *Salt and freshly ground black*
1 clove garlic, crushed   *pepper*

1. Put all the ingredients in a bowl and toss to coat.
2. Pile into a salad bowl and set aside until ready to serve or serve immediately.

A Birthday Celebration

Serves 6

A dinner party for six with a sumptuous birthday cake that can be made in a flash. Most large supermarkets now sell tubs of ready prepared seafood (prawns, mussels, crab sticks and cockles) or they have a deli where it can be bought. This starter may be prepared up to 1½ hours in advance. Simply refrigerate the combined seafood and dressing in one bowl and assemble the starters when just about ready to serve.

Menu

Mixed Seafood Cocktail

~ ● ~

Pork Fillet Normandy
Basmati Rice (*see page 68*)

~ ● ~

Herby Carrots

~ ● ~

Boozy Chocolate Birthday Cake

Order

1. Make the cake up to 4 days in advance and keep wrapped in fridge.
2. About 40 minutes before the meal, soak the rice, then prepare the starters and refrigerate, covered.
3. Prepare the carrots. Next make the pork dish, cover and leave standing. Add the cream as you re-heat.
4. Lastly, turn out the chocolate cake and top with the creamy fromage frais.
5. The carrots and rice are cooked whilst you eat the starter and the pork re-heated between courses.

Mixed Seafood Cocktail

Preparation time: 10 mins
Cooking time: 0

*1 bag ready prepared salad
   leaves*
*100g (4oz) baby tomatoes,
   halved*
*750g (1¹/₂lb) prepared, cooked
   seafood (prawns, mussels,
   crab sticks and cockles)*
1 clove garlic, crushed
30ml (2 tablespoons) olive oil
Juice of ¹/₂ lime

*15ml (1 tablespoon) freshly
   chopped parsley*
*Salt and freshly ground black
   pepper*
*60ml (4 tablespoons) reduced
   calorie mayonnaise*
5ml (1 teaspoon) tomato purée
*45ml (3 tablespoons) fromage
   frais*
Ground paprika

To serve
wedges of lemon

basket of bread rolls and butter

1. Divide the salad leaves and baby tomatoes between six individual serving plates.
2. Put the prepared seafood into a mixing bowl. Add the garlic, olive oil and lime juice with the chopped parsley. Season lightly. Toss to mix.
3. Put the mayonnaise into a mixing bowl. Add the tomato purée and the fromage frais, with a little seasoning. Stir to combine.
4. Top the salads evenly with the seafood mixture. Add a . spoonful of mayonnaise mixture to each one and serve immediately, garnished with a wedge of lemon and a light dusting of paprika on the mayonnaise.

Pork Fillet Normandy

Preparation time: 10 mins
Cooking time: 18 mins

*1 medium dessert apple
  (preferably Cox's)
550ml (1 pint) medium sweet
  cider
30ml (2 tablespoons) rape seed
  oil*

*1 onion, chopped
750g (1¹/₂lb) pork fillet, cut
  into thin strips
7.5ml (¹/₂ tablespoon)
  cornflour
150ml (5 fl oz) whipping cream*

1. Peel, core and slice the apple, putting the core and peel into a medium saucepan. Pour the cider over the peel and bring the pan to the boil (it's quicker if you cover it with a lid). Remove lid and simmer the cider fairly rapidly until it is reduced by about half – this should take about 5–7 minutes.
2. Heat the oil in a large frying pan or wok and fry the onion until golden. Add the pork and stir-fry for 7–9 minutes, until golden.
3. Stir in the apple slices. Add the strained, reduced cider. Mix cornflour to a smooth paste with a little water and stir into the pan.
4. Bring to the boil, stirring. Simmer gently for 1–2 minutes.
5. Stir in the cream and re-heat to serve.

Herby Carrots

Preparation time: 5 mins
Cooking time: 10 mins

*750g (1¹/2lb) tender young
  carrots, with their tops on if
  possible*

*45ml (3 tablespoons) olive oil
15ml (1 tablespoon) freshly
  chopped mixed herbs*

1. Scrub the carrots clean, trimming the tops if necessary.
2. Put them into a pan with about 300ml (10 fl oz) water. Simmer until tender, about 8–10 minutes.
3. Drain and return to pan. Add olive oil and herbs. Toss to coat. Serve immediately.

Boozy Chocolate Birthday Cake

This cake is sheer indulgence and couldn't be called healthy by any stretch of the imagination. However, occasionally a little of what you fancy does you good, so enjoy a small portion and don't feel too guilty!

Preparation time: 15 mins + chilling time
Cooking time: 5 mins

25g (1oz) raisins
30ml (2 tablespoons) rum
1 × 200g (7oz) bar good
   quality dark chocolate
100g (4oz) butter, cut into
   pieces

1 × 397g (14oz) can sweetened
   condensed milk
275g (10oz) ginger biscuits,
   roughly broken (not
   crushed)
50g (2oz) glacé cherries,
   washed and chopped

To serve:
150ml (5 fl oz) fromage frais
stem ginger, in syrup, drained
   and sliced

4 ripe pears, peeled and sliced

1. Put the raisins into a cup. Pour over the rum and leave to soak while you melt the chocolate.
2. Break the chocolate into pieces and put into a large, heavy-based pan. Add the butter and the condensed milk. Heat gently, until melted, stirring occasionally. Stir in broken biscuits, raisins and any remaining rum with the glacé cherries.
3. Line a 20cm (8in) round, shallow loose-bottomed cake tin with aluminium foil to cover base and come up and overlap sides. Pour mixture into tin evenly, then chill until firm (a minimum of 4 hours in the fridge, but you could speed things up by putting it into the freezer for a couple of hours).
4. Turn onto flat serving plate. Peel away foil.
5. Spread fromage frais over top of cake. Decorate with the sliced ginger and serve with the fresh pears.
   Note: This cake should be cut with a sharp knife dipped into hot water then dried.

Valentine's Day

Serves 2

This stunning meal needs little last minute attention. The redcurrant sauce and the raspberries are bright red for a bit of romance. An easy menu, fit to turn anyone's head. A soft white Italian wine such as Pinot Grigio would be ideal with the starter, then perhaps Chianti with the lamb.

Menu

Smoked Mackerel with Horseradish
~ • ~
Butterfly Lamb Chops with Redcurrant Jelly Sauce
Mangetout Peas with Sweetcorn
Buttered Noodles
~ • ~
Ice Cream Dreams

Order

1. About 40 minutes before the meal, prepare the fruit for the desserts. Leave, covered in the fridge, completing the sundaes on serving.
2. Next, make the sauce for the chops – it can be re-heated after you've eaten the starter, which you prepare next and put on the table.
3. Lastly, grill the chops and stir-fry the veg, undercooking these slightly as you can put both chops and veg onto a serving dish, cover loosely with foil and hold in a low oven for up to 15 minutes while you enjoy the starter.
4. Simmer the noodles, according to directions on the packet. Re-heat redcurrant sauce. Drain and toss noodles in a knob of butter on serving.

Smoked Mackerel with Horseradish

A quick-to-assemble starter that's high on taste and fairly filling, too. Serve with granary bread.

Preparation time: 10 mins
Cooking time: 0

4 leaves of frisee lettuce
6 black olives
1 × 215g pack (7¹/₂oz) chilled smoked mackerel selection (selection consists of 2 fillets mackerel and 2 fillets peppered smoked mackerel)

30ml (2 tablespoons) creamed horseradish
2 wedges lemon

1. Wash and drain the lettuce well, then tear it up and divide between 2 medium-sized plates.
2. Add the olives, then add one fillet of each type of mackerel.
3. Add 15ml (1 tablespoon) horseradish to the side of each plate. Garnish with the lemon wedges and serve.

Butterfly Lamb Chops with Redcurrant Jelly Sauce

Preparation time: 10 mins
Cooking time: 12 mins

Olive oil, for brushing

For the sauce

150ml (5 fl oz) dry white wine
30ml (2 tablespoons) redcurrant jelly
10ml (2 teaspoons) clear honey
5ml (1 teaspoon) dried parsley

2 British lamb butterfly chops

Salt and freshly ground black pepper
5ml (1 teaspoon) cornflour
100g (4oz) fresh or frozen redcurrants (optional)

To serve
2 sprigs of fresh or frozen redcurrants

1. Oil the rack and pre-heat the grill to a medium heat.
2. Trim any visible fat from the chops and discard.
3. Cook the chops on one side for about 7 minutes, turn over and continue to cook for a further 5–6 minutes, until cooked.
4. Meanwhile, prepare the sauce. Put the wine, redcurrant jelly, honey and parsley into a medium-sized pan. Season with salt and pepper. Add the cornflour. Stir well.
5. Heat, stirring, until sauce boils and thickens. Stir in the redcurrants, if using, and re-heat gently.
6. To serve, arrange the chops on individual serving plates, spooning a little of the sauce over. Garnish each plate with a sprig of redcurrants. Serve remaining sauce separately.

Mangetout Peas with Sweetcorn

Preparation time: 5 mins
Cooking time: 5 mins

30ml (2 tablespoons) olive oil
175g (6oz) baby sweetcorn, halved lengthways
175g (6oz) mangetout, topped and tailed

1. Heat the oil in a large frying pan. Add the corn and the mangetout and stir-fry for 3–4 minutes, until tender.
2. Serve immediately.

Ice Cream Dreams

Preparation time: 10 mins + soaking time
Cooking time: 0

2 kiwi fruits
225g (8oz) raspberries
60ml (4 tablespoons) Sauternes
  or other medium sweet white
  wine
2 scoops vanilla ice cream

10ml (2 teaspoons) runny
  honey
25g (1oz) toasted flaked
  almonds
2 fancy ice cream wafers

1. Peel and thinly slice the kiwi fruits. Divide slices between two sundae dishes. Add the raspberries.
2. Spoon 30ml (2 tablespoons) wine over the fruit in each dish. Cover and chill for 15 minutes or so.
3. On serving, top each dessert with a scoop of ice cream. Drizzle honey over ice cream.
4. Top with nuts and decorate with wafers.

Mother's Day Treat

Serves 4

Let the children help with this meal which is easy to prepare and serve. Teenagers should be able to make this treat on their own.

Menu

Speedy Thai Soup (optional)
Chicken Breast Parcels
Baked Potatoes with Soured Cream & Chives
Garden Salad
~ • ~
Special Danish Pastries

Order

1. About 1 hour before you want to eat, start by pre-heating the oven and when hot (after 15 minutes or so), bake the prepared potatoes on a high shelf.
2. Prepare the Danish pastries and bake.
3. Prepare the chicken parcels next and pop them into the oven as soon as the pastries are cooked.
4. Prepare the salad and chill in the fridge, don't add dressing until ready to serve. Prepare the soup, if using.
5. Ice the pastries as soon as they cool a little.
6. On serving, add dressing to salad. Toss to coat and serve.
7. Serve chicken parcels with potatoes.

Speedy Thai Soup

Speedy and fragrant, this delicious soup is simplicity itself to prepare and cook. If you have to defrost the prawns, add any resulting liquid to the soup.

Preparation time: 10 mins
Cooking time: 10 mins

1 litre (1³/₄ pints) chicken stock
6 spring onions, roughly chopped
1.25–2.5ml (¹/₄–¹/₂ teaspoon) hot chilli powder
2.5ml (¹/₂ teaspoon) ground coriander
2 cloves garlic, crushed
5ml (1 teaspoon) lemon juice
30ml (2 tablespoons) fresh basil leaves, torn
15ml (1 tablespoon) dry sherry
15ml (1 tablespoon) fish sauce
15ml (1 tablespoon) soy sauce
15ml (1 tablespoon) cornflour
175g (6oz) frozen sweetcorn
350g (12oz) large shelled prawns, defrosted if frozen

1. Put the stock into a large saucepan. Add the spring onions with the chilli powder, coriander, garlic, lemon juice, basil, sherry, fish sauce and soy sauce.
2. Blend the cornflour to a smooth paste with 30ml (2 tablespoons) water and stir into the saucepan. Add the sweetcorn.

3. Bring to the boil, stirring. Simmer, covered, for 5 minutes.
4. Add the prawns and return to heat until thoroughly hot, but don't boil the soup again. Serve immediately.

Chicken Breast Parcels

You will need four pieces of foil, each about 27.5cm (11in) square.

Preparation time: 10 mins
Cooking time: 30 mins

4 even-sized skinned fresh chicken breast fillets, about 200g (7oz) each
4 thin slices lean smoked ham
350g (12oz) baby sweetcorn, fresh or frozen
16 mangetout, trimmed
2 large sticks celery, chopped finely

4 dried apricots, chopped with scissors
40ml (4 tablespoons) dry white wine or cider
10ml (2 teaspoons) dried basil
Salt and freshly ground black pepper

1. Pre-heat the oven to 400°F (200°C) gas mark 6, while you prepare the chicken.
2. Spread the pieces of foil out individually on the worktop.
3. Wrap each breast of chicken in a piece of ham and arrange in the centre of the foil squares.
4. Divide sweetcorn, mangetout and celery into four and add to the chicken. Add one snipped dried apricot to each parcel. Pour 15ml (1 tablespoon) wine or cider over each chicken breast, then add the basil and season lightly with salt and pepper.
5. Gather up edges of foil and seal to make four loose bundles. Place on a baking sheet.
6. Bake for 30 minutes, until chicken is cooked. To test chicken, carefully unwrap a parcel and pierce breast with a sharp knife

- any juices should run clear. If pink juices run out, seal parcel up and return to oven for a further 5 minutes, then test again.
7. Serve the chicken with its vegetables and juices, accompanied by the garden salad and baked potatoes.

Baked Potatoes

New potatoes are delicious baked in their skins and are very easy to cook.

Preparation time: 10 mins
Cooking time: 30–40 mins

12 medium-sized new potatoes   *Salt and freshly ground black*
About 30ml (2 tablespoons)   *pepper*
  olive oil

To serve
150ml (5 fl oz) soured cream   *snipped chives*

1. Pre-heat the oven to 400°F (200°C) gas mark 6.
2. Scrub potatoes clean then blot dry on absorbent kitchen paper. Pierce each one once with a knife or a fork. Put into a roasting tin.
3. Brush the potatoes lightly with oil and sprinkle with salt and pepper.
4. Bake the potatoes for 30–40 minutes, until tender. To test, pierce centre of potatoes with a sharp knife – they should give easily.
5. Serve immediately with the soured cream offered separately, topped with a few snipped chives.

Garden Salad

Preparation time: 10 mins
Cooking time: 0

*1× 100g (4oz) bag Continental
    mixed salad leaves*

*1 carton mustard and cress
¹/2 ripe avocado*

For the dressing

*75ml (5 tablespoons) olive oil
30ml (2 tablespoons) lemon
    vinegar*

*5ml (1 teaspoon) dried parsley
Salt and freshly ground black
    pepper*

1. Empty the bag of leaves into a salad bowl. Snip off the mustard and cress with scissors and add to the bowl.
2. Peel and slice the avocado and add to the bowl.
3. Prepare the dressing. Put the oil into a mug with the vinegar, parsley and a little seasoning. Whisk briefly with a fork, then pour over the salad. Toss with two spoons and serve immediately.

Special Danish Pastries

The pack of Danish pastries comes complete with icing.

Preparation time: 10 mins
Cooking time: 15 mins

*1× 306g (11oz) can Pillsbury
    Danish Whirls
30ml (2 tablespoons) clear
    honey (warmed in the
    microwave for 15 seconds)*

*1.25ml (¹/4 teaspoon)
    cinnamon
6 glacé cherries, chopped
15g (¹/2oz) flaked almonds or
    almond nibs*

1. Pre-heat the oven to 400°F (200°C) gas mark 6.
2. Carefully unroll dough, keeping it in one piece.
3. Brush honey over surface of dough. Sprinkle with cinnamon.

4. Re-roll, making sure the perforations are straight.
5. Cut into 6 pastries, using perforations as a guide, and place on greased baking sheet.
6. Press cherries and almonds on top of pastries and bake for 13–15 minutes, until golden brown and cooked through.
7. Rest for 3 minutes, then drizzle icing onto pastries from a teaspoon. Serve warm or cold.

Easy Easter

Serves 6

A springtime, two-course lunch or dinner menu to serve over Easter. The poached salmon is probably the easiest main course dish you'll ever cook!

Menu

Whole Poached Salmon
Orange & Cucumber Salad
Buttered New Potatoes
Red Pepper, Celery & Pine Nut Salad
Parsley & Mustard Blender Mayonnaise
~ • ~

Mango Cheesecake with Pouring Cream

Order

1. Prepare and cook salmon well in advance. Leave in poaching liquid to cool completely.
2. Prepare and chill mango cheesecake well in advance.
3. 40 minutes before you want to serve the meal, prepare the chick pea salad. Cover and place on table.
4. 30 minutes before the meal, make the mayonnaise.
5. Prepare the orange and cucumber salad next, leaving the dressing in a jug beside it, to be added on serving.
6. 20 minutes before the meal, cook the new potatoes while you serve and garnish the salmon. Transfer the cheesecake to a serving plate.

Whole Poached Salmon

A wonderful fish to serve for a special occasion. If you have a bottle of either white or red wine already open, use 150ml (5 fl oz) wine in place of some of the water used to poach the fish.

You will need a roasting dish and two large pieces of aluminium foil or a fish kettle with a lid.

Preparation time: 10 mins
Cooking time: 8 mins **+** 2 hours standing

1× 2–2.25kg (4–5lb) whole salmon, gutted and cleaned
2 medium carrots, chopped
1 stick celery, chopped

1 medium onion, sliced
Small bunch parsley, tied with string
15ml (1 tablespoon) salt

To garnish
lettuce
slices of cucumber

parsley
lemon wedges

1. Remove the gills at the back of the head of the salmon, then put the fish into the fish kettle or roasting tin (grease the roasting tin with a little olive oil first). If using a roasting tin, cut the fish into two halves, vertically through the middle, then arrange both halves side by side in the tin.
2. Carefully pour in approx. 1.5–1.75 litres (2½–3 pints) cold water (enough to come three-quarters of the way up the salmon), then add all remaining ingredients.
3. Stand tin on hob and heat slowly to simmering point.
4. As soon as the first bubbles appear, turn the heat down, cover the pan completely with the lid or a large sheet of foil, then leave fish to poach for 8 minutes.
5. Remove pan from heat and set aside, covered, until cold (at least 2 hours). The fish will now be perfectly cooked.
6. Carefully lift the fish onto a large piece of foil.
7. Peel off the skin (it comes away very easily). Roll the fish over, using the foil and remove skin from other side, as well as any creamy brown bits that occur which simply need scraping away gently with a knife.
8. Using the foil again, carefully roll the salmon onto a serving dish. (If you cut the fish in half, join it back together again and hide the join with garnish.)
9. Fill sides of the dish with plenty of shredded lettuce then put a single layer of thinly sliced cucumber right down the centre of

the fish, overlapping the slices. Complete garnish with parsley and lemon wedges before serving.
10. To serve salmon, cut wedges from either side of bone on top of the fish, then lift out bone and serve remaining salmon.

Orange & Cucumber Salad

Preparation time: 10–15 mins
Cooking time: 0

4¹/₂ oranges   *¹/₂ cucumber*

For the dressing

Juice of ¹/₂ orange   *15ml (1 tablespoon) freshly*
30ml (2 tablespoons) red wine   *chopped mint*
vinegar   *120ml (8 tablespoons) olive oil*
Salt and freshly ground black
pepper

To garnish
tiny sprigs of fresh mint

1. Peel and segment the oranges, discarding pith and membrane and holding the fruit over a small bowl to catch any juice that drips out. Put into serving bowl.
2. Slice the cucumber and add to the serving bowl.
3. Make the dressing. Add the juice of the ¹/₂ orange to the drips of juice already in the small bowl. Add the vinegar and season lightly with salt and pepper. Add the mint and olive oil and whisk with a fork.
4. Just before serving, pour the dressing onto the salad. Toss to coat. Garnish with the sprigs of mint.

Buttered New Potatoes

Preparation time: 7 mins
Cooking time: 15 mins

1kg (2lb) tiny new potatoes,
  scrubbed clean
2 sprigs of fresh mint

50g (2oz) butter
30ml (2 tablespoons) freshly
  chopped parsley and mint

1. Cook the new potatoes in a covered pan of boiling water with the mint for about 15 minutes, until just tender. Drain and return to pan, discarding mint.
2. Add butter and herbs to the pan and shake gently until butter melts. Serve immediately.

Red Pepper, Celery & Pine Nut Salad

Preparation time: 15 mins
Cooking time: 5 mins

6 sticks celery, chopped
2 medium red peppers, halved
  and seeded

1 bunch spring onions,
  chopped
1× 430g (15oz) can chick
  peas, drained

For the apple dressing

5ml (1 teaspoon) grated lemon
  rind
75ml (5 tablespoons) olive oil
30ml (2 tablespoons) apple
  juice

15ml (1 tablespoon) freshly
  chopped oregano
Salt and freshly ground black
  pepper

To serve
a few chopped celery leaves

50g (2oz) pine nuts, toasted

1. Put the chopped celery into a large salad bowl.
2. Heat the peppers, skin side up, under a moderate grill until the skins blacken. Allow to cool, then peel the peppers (this is

much easier than it sounds). Slice the skinned peppers and
add to the bowl.

3. Add the spring onions and the drained chick peas.
4. Prepare the dressing. Put the lemon rind into a small bowl.
   Add the olive oil and the apple juice with the oregano.
   Season with a little salt and pepper. Whisk lightly with a fork.
5. Pour the dressing over the salad and toss to coat. Allow to
   stand for 5–10 minutes for flavours to mingle. Serve topped
   with a few chopped celery leaves and sprinkled with the
   toasted pine nuts.

Parsley & Mustard Blender Mayonnaise

Don't worry if you want to make this and haven't cooked the
fish. The mayonnaise will be fine without the fish juices.

Preparation time: 10 mins
Cooking time: 0

1 egg, size 2
1 egg yolk, size 2
300ml (10 fl oz) olive oil
*30ml (2 tablespoons) lemon
  juice*
*Salt and freshly ground black
  pepper*

45ml (3 tablespoons) fish juices
*10ml (2 teaspoons) granary
  mustard*
*30ml (2 tablespoons) freshly
  chopped parsley*

1. Put the egg and egg yolk into the food processor. Process
   using the metal blade for about 20 seconds.
2. With the machine running, start to trickle the oil in through
   the feed tube using the hole to drip-feed it in, if you have one.
   It is important that the oil is added a tiny amount at a time to
   begin with, until an emulsion is formed. Continue until a
   thick mayonnaise results and all the oil has been added (about
   1 minute).
3. Add the lemon juice, seasoning and the fish juices, and
   process for a further 20 seconds.

4. Fold in the granary mustard with the parsley and use immediately.
   Note: Should there be any mayonnaise left over, it will keep for a few days refrigerated in an airtight container.

Mango Cheesecake with Pouring Cream

A wonderfully light, tangy cheesecake without too many calories. If you haven't time to pipe cream, simply decorate with tiny sprigs of fresh mint.

Preparation time: 15 mins
Cooking time: 5 mins + 40 mins chilling time

75g (3oz) butter
125g (5oz) digestive biscuits,
   crushed

25g (1oz) pecan nuts, chopped

For the cheesecake topping

1 × 11g (¼oz) packet gelatine
225g (8oz) reduced fat cream
   cheese
2 mangoes, peeled and roughly
   chopped, discarding central
   stone

275g (10oz) fromage frais
2 eggs, size 2, separated
50g (2oz) caster sugar

To decorate
150ml (5 fl oz) whipping cream (optional)

To serve
single cream

1. Melt the butter in a medium-sized saucepan. Stir the biscuits and nuts into the melted butter. Press mixture into base of lightly greased 20cm (8in) loose-bottomed cake tin.
2. Put 60ml (4 tablespoons) water into a bowl. Sprinkle over the gelatine and set aside for 10 minutes. Place bowl over a pan of

gently simmering water and stir until dissolved. Set aside to cool.

3. Put the cream cheese into the food processor. Add half the mango flesh and process using the metal blade until smooth. Add the fromage frais and the egg yolks. Process just to combine.

4. Remove blade from processor. Add sugar and remaining mango and fold in gently. Stir dissolved gelatine in swiftly and evenly. Turn into large mixing bowl.

5. In a clean mixing bowl, beat egg whites until stiff and fold into the mango mixture using a metal spoon.

6. Pour filling over biscuit base. Refrigerate for about 40 minutes until set.

7. Decorate with piped, whipped cream if using, before serving with a jug of single cream.

Alternative Christmas Dinner

Serves 8

Everyone loves chicken and this spicy version will prove especially popular. The mango sauce has a delicious tang and is served chilled for ease. A fishy starter and two fruity desserts complete the meal which is fit for any feast!

Prepare and freeze the ice cream up to one month in advance and marinate the chicken the day before.

Menu

Crab, Corn & Celery Salads
Spiced Chicken with Mango Sauce
New Potatoes in Mustard Vinaigrette
Broccoli with Garlic Crumbs (*see page 65*)
~ ● ~
Fruits in Kirsch
Chocolate, Apricot & Ginger Ice Cream (*see page 160*)

Order

1. About 1¹/₂ hours before the meal, pre-heat the oven for the chicken.
2. Prepare the fruits in Kirsch. Cover and chill. Prepare starters. Chill.
3. 40 minutes before you want to serve the starters, cook the chicken.
4. Prepare vegetables, putting them on to cook just before you serve the starters.
5. Prepare the mango sauce.
6. Serve starters as the chicken is cooked, so that it can be left to stand, covered, for 10 minutes to relax.

Individual Crab, Corn & Celery Salads

These salads may be made up to 1 hour in advance and kept covered in the refrigerator.

Preparation time: 10 mins
Cooking time: 5 mins

175g (8oz) frozen sweetcorn kernels
3 long sticks celery, finely chopped
60ml (4 tablespoons) reduced fat mayonnaise
45ml (3 tablespoons) fromage frais
15ml (1 tablespoon) tomato ketchup

10ml (2 teaspoons) lemon juice
Salt and freshly ground black pepper
¹/₂ Iceberg lettuce, shredded
2× 170g (6oz) cans white crab meat
225g (8oz) prawns, defrosted if frozen

To garnish
wedges of lemon   *sprigs of dill*

1. Cook the sweetcorn in a little boiling water for 5 minutes. Drain through a sieve and rinse with cold water. Turn into a large mixing bowl. Alternatively, if you have a microwave,

put sweetcorn into a soup bowl. Cover with cling film and microwave on 100%/FULL power for 5 minutes. Stir and turn into mixing bowl. Allow to cool.
2. Add the celery to the bowl.
3. Blend together the mayonnaise, fromage frais, tomato ketchup and lemon juice. Season and fold in the dill. Turn onto sweetcorn mixture and toss to coat.
4. Arrange the lettuce on eight serving dishes. Top with the sweetcorn mixture. Top with the crab meat and prawns, and serve immediately garnished with the wedges of lemon and the sprigs of dill.

Spiced Chicken with Mango Sauce

Preparation time: 10 mins
Cooking time: 35–40 mins

8 part-boned, fresh chicken breasts, skin removed
10ml (2 teaspoons) medium Madras curry powder
45ml (3 tablespoons) tomato purée

90ml (6 tablespoons) olive oil
75ml (5 tablespoons) red wine
2 cloves garlic, crushed
10ml (2 teaspoons) tarragon
Salt and freshly ground black pepper

For the sauce

1 large ripe mango
45ml (3 tablespoons) mango chutney
225g (8oz) Greek yoghurt

2 spring onions, chopped
5ml (1 teaspoon) lemon juice
Salt and freshly ground black pepper

To garnish
slices of mango

fresh coriander leaves

1. Slash each chicken breast three times with a sharp knife, making fairly shallow cuts. Arrange in a shallow dish in a single layer.

2. In a mixing bowl, combine curry powder, tomato purée, olive oil, red wine, garlic and tarragon. Season with a little salt and pepper. Mix well.
3. Spoon spicy mixture over chicken. Cover and leave to marinate for 2 hours, or overnight. (Turn chicken in marinade once or twice, if possible.)
4. About 1 hour before you want to serve, pre-heat oven to 425°F (220°C) gas mark 7.
5. Lift chicken portions onto a roasting rack arranged in roasting tin. Spoon over any extra marinade.
6. Bake chicken for approx. 35–40 minutes, until well browned and tender, basting the chicken occasionally. The chicken is cooked when juices run clear when chicken is pierced with a sharp knife. Set aside for 10 minutes to relax.
7. Meanwhile, make the sauce. Peel the mango, then slice flesh away from central flat stone. Roughly chop the flesh and put it into the food processor with the chutney and yoghurt. Process until smooth.
8. Stir the spring onions and lemon juice into the mango sauce. Season with salt and pepper to taste. Cover and chill until ready to serve.
9. Serve the chicken garnished with the fresh mango slices and sprigs of coriander, handing the cold sauce round separately.

New Potatoes in Mustard Vinaigrette

Preparation time: 10 mins
Cooking time: 15–20 mins

1kg (2lb) new potatoes, scrubbed clean
30ml (2 tablespoons) wholegrain mustard

45ml (3 tablespoons) olive oil
Salt and freshly ground black pepper

1. Boil or steam the potatoes for 15–20 minutes, until tender.
2. Whisk the mustard into the olive oil. Season lightly.

3. Return the drained potatoes to a saucepan. Add the mustard mixture. Toss to coat. Serve immediately.

Fruits in Kirsch

Frozen redcurrants work well in this recipe.

Preparation time: 10 mins
Cooking time: 0

6 oranges
225g (8oz) fresh strawberries
225g (8oz) redcurrants,
    removed from stem

About 15ml (1 tablespoon)
    caster sugar
90ml (6 tablespoons) Kirsch,
    Grand Marnier or Cointreau

To serve
whipped cream or Greek yoghurt

1. Peel oranges, removing all pith then segment the fruits, holding them over a shallow serving dish, so that you catch any juice.
2. Put the orange segments into the serving dish.
3. Wash, hull and slice the strawberries. Add to the oranges. Add the redcurrants.
4. Sprinkle with sugar and pour liqueur over.
5. Cover and chill until ready to serve (15 minutes is long enough for flavours to mingle). Serve with whipped cream or Greek yoghurt.

New Year's Eve Fork Supper

Serves 6

Welcome the New Year in style. This attractive supper menu can be organised well in advance, completing the menu at the last minute with no effort at all. Serve a selection of wines, including a sparkling one.

Menu

Wine Glazed Salmon Steaks
Broad Bean & Sun-dried Tomato Salad
Risotto with Kidney Beans, Apricots & Cashew Nuts (*see page 169*)
Festive Coleslaw
Half-baked Frozen Wholemeal Baguettes
or
French Bread
~ ● ~
Cheese Board
Pears in Wine & Port with Ginger Cream

Order

1. About 1 hour before the meal, prepare the pears and bake them in the oven. Prepare cream and chill until ready to serve.
2. Then prepare and glaze the salmon; set it to one side to be grilled when ready to serve.
3. Next, prepare the coleslaw and chill, covered.
4. 40 minutes before eating, prepare the risotto and while it cooks, arrange the cheese on the board with grapes, celery and walnuts. You may like to use Scottish cheeses only for New Year and include some oat cakes with the crackers.

5. 10 minutes before serving, bake the baguettes according to instructions on the packet.
6. Re-heat the risotto over gentle heat, stirring occasionally.
7. Grill the salmon just before serving.

Wine Glazed Salmon Steaks

Preparation time: 5 mins + marinating time
Cooking time: 8 mins

*6 salmon cutlets, about 175g
(6oz) each*

For the glaze

*15ml (1 tablespoon) olive oil
15ml (1 tablespoon) clear
honey
5ml (1 teaspoon) dried basil*

*5ml (1 teaspoon) tomato purée
Salt and freshly ground black
pepper*

To garnish
wedges of lemon

1. Prepare the glaze. Put all ingredients for the glaze into a mug and whisk, using a fork to blend.
2. Arrange salmon steaks in a single layer in a suitable shallow dish. Brush all over with the glaze.
3. Cover and set aside for 10 minutes, or can be covered and refrigerated for up to 3 hours.
4. When ready to cook, pre-heat the grill to medium hot then line the grill pan with foil.
5. Arrange salmon on the foil and grill for approx. 4 minutes each side, until cooked.
6. Serve immediately, arranged on an oval dish, with the fish juices poured over, garnished with wedges of lemon.

Broad Bean & Sun-dried Tomato Salad

Preparation time: 5 mins
Cooking time: 8 mins

1kg (2lb) frozen broad beans
75g (3oz) sun-dried tomatoes
in olive oil
150ml (5 fl oz) natural yoghurt
5ml (1 teaspoon) good quality
commercially-made mint
sauce

Salt and freshly ground black
pepper
25g (1oz) toasted flaked
almonds

1. Cook the beans in boiling water for 6–8 minutes, according to directions on the packet. Drain and turn into large mixing bowl. Leave to cool.
2. Drain and slice tomatoes and add to the cooled beans.
3. Blend the yoghurt with the mint sauce and season lightly with salt and pepper.
4. Pour yoghurt dressing over beans. Toss to coat.
5. Turn into serving dish and serve, sprinkled with the toasted almonds.

Festive Coleslaw

Red and green foods look colourful and appetising. There's plenty of crunch in this lightly curry-flavoured salad.

Preparation time: 15 mins
Cooking time: 0

225g (8oz) red cabbage
350g (12oz) green cabbage
225g (8oz) carrots, grated
1 small, young leek, thinly
sliced

50g (2oz) dried apricots,
chopped
50g (2oz) dried cranberries
with cherries or 50g (2oz)
dates, stoned and chopped

For the dressing

150ml (5 fl oz) Greek yoghurt
Grated rind of ¹/₂ orange
Juice of 1 orange
2.5ml (¹/₂ teaspoon) curry
  powder

15ml (1 tablespoon) freshly
  chopped basil
Salt and freshly ground black
  pepper

1. Shred the red and green cabbage finely using the shredding disc on a food processor, if available.
2. Put into a large mixing bowl. Add the carrot and leek with the apricots, cranberries and cherries or dates.
3. Prepare the dressing. Put all ingredients for the dressing into a jug. Blend until smooth.
4. Pour dressing onto salad and toss lightly to coat.
5. Check seasoning. Turn into serving dish and chill until ready to serve.

Pears in Wine & Port with Ginger Cream

Preparation time: 10 mins
Cooking time: 30–35 mins

6 large, ripe pears
200ml (7 fl oz) red wine
45ml (3 tablespoons) port

30ml (2 tablespoons) clear
  honey
1 cinnamon stick
4 cloves

1. Pre-heat the oven to 375°F (190°C) gas mark 5.
2. Peel the pears, leaving the stalks in place.
3. Stand them in a 1.75 litre (3 pint) fairly shallow dish.
4. Mix the wine with the port and honey, and pour over pears. Add cinnamon stick and cloves.
5. Bake for 30–35 minutes, until tender. Serve immediately with the ginger cream (see opposite).

Ginger Cream

Preparation time: 5 mins
Cooking time: 0

*150ml (5 fl oz) whipping
  cream*
150ml (5 fl oz) fromage frais

*10ml (2 teaspoons) caster sugar
5ml (1 teaspoon) grated root
  ginger*

1. Put the cream into a mixing bowl and whip until standing in soft peaks.
2. Fold in the fromage frais, caster sugar and the ginger.
3. Turn into serving dish, cover and refrigerate until ready to use.

Fast Finger Buffet

Serves 12

An easy, tasty finger buffet that can be put together quickly. Serve red and white wine and perhaps a jug of Bucks Fizz (sparkling wine or champagne and orange juice).

Menu

Crunchy herb-flavoured meze sticks (available from large delis and good supermarkets)
350g (12oz) hummus (buy from a good deli counter)
350g (12oz) taramasalata (buy from a good deli counter)
Fresh sticks of carrot, celery, red pepper, whole radish
Double recipe of Dates with Bacon (*see page 45*)
Cheese Balls
Spiced Cocktail Nuts (*see page 46*)
Prawn & Crab Stuffed Tomatoes
Cheesy Tomato Bread Twists
Salmon with Peach Dipping Sauce

Order

1. About 1½ hours before serving, prepare tomatoes, leave upside down to drain. Prepare filling. Set aside.
2. Prepare the cheese balls next.
3. Grill the nuts and toss in seasoning. Put into serving dish.
4. About 45 minutes before serving, prepare and grill the tapas.
5. Prepare vegetable sticks and put dips in bowls, and meze sticks on a colourful plate. Grill the salmon and make the peach sauce.
6. Fill drained tomatoes and serve.
7. Make the cheesy tomato bread twists and serve warm.

Cheese Balls
Makes 30 cheese balls

Preparation time: 15 mins
Cooking time: 0

175g (6oz) Cheddar cheese
175g (6oz) Red Leicester
 cheese
2 small sticks celery and 1 sprig
 celery leaves, finely chopped

2 spring onions, finely
 chopped
Cayenne pepper
Few drops chilli sauce
75ml (5 tablespoons)
 mayonnaise

To serve
75g (3oz) toasted almond nibs

5ml (1 teaspoon) paprika
 pepper

1. Grate the Cheddar cheese and the Red Leicester cheese into a large mixing bowl.
2. Add the celery and spring onion. Season lightly with a pinch of cayenne.
3. Add chilli sauce and mayonnaise and mix well to combine. Taste and add a little more chilli sauce, if required.
4. Combine almond nibs and paprika on a dinner plate.
5. Roll teaspoons of the mixture into balls. Roll in almonds to coat and arrange on serving plate. Serve or chill until ready to serve.

Prawn & Crab Stuffed Tomatoes

Preparation time: 25 mins
Cooking time: 0

12 smallish English tomatoes
 (not cherry)
Salt and freshly ground black
 pepper

1 × 170g (5³/₄oz) can white
 crab meat
15ml (1 tablespoon) freshly
 chopped parsley

225g (8oz) peeled prawns,
　defrosted if frozen, chopped
30ml (2 tablespoons)
　mayonnaise

15ml (1 tablespoon) fromage
　frais
5ml (1 teaspoon) tomato purée

To serve
mustard and cress

1. Cut the top off each tomato and, using a teaspoon, carefully scoop out core and seeds and discard. Sprinkle insides of tomatoes with a little salt, then stand upside down on a tray and set aside to drain for 10 minutes.
2. Put the crab meat into a large mixing bowl. Add the parsley and prawns.
3. Blend together the mayonnaise, fromage frais and the tomato purée. Season with the salt and pepper. Add to crab meat. Mix gently to combine.
4. Turn drained tomatoes right side up and fill with fish mixture.
5. Arrange mustard and cress on serving dish and top with filled tomatoes. Serve.

Cheesy Tomato Bread Twists

Pillsbury crispy white bread twists are available from the chill counter of your supermarket. You will need three baking sheets.

Preparation time: 10 mins
Cooking time: 10 mins

2 × 192g (6¹/₂oz) cans
　Pillsbury crispy white bread
　twists
30ml (2 tablespoons) tomato
　purée

Freshly ground black pepper
75g (3oz) mature Cheddar
　cheese, finely grated

To serve
Approx. 15ml (1 tablespoon) grated Parmesan cheese

1. Pre-heat the oven to 375°F (190°C) gas mark 5.
2. Unroll both tubes of dough gently. Separate each roll of dough at the perforations to form 10 strips. You will have 20 strips of dough.
3. Spread each strip with tomato purée, then season with a little black pepper. Sprinkle with Cheddar cheese, then twist each strip of dough carefully, stretching it slightly and pressing on any cheese that falls off.
4. Place well apart on ungreased baking sheets, pressing ends well down.
5. Bake for 10–12 minutes, until golden. Serve warm if possible, sprinkled with the grated Parmesan.

Salmon with Peach Dipping Sauce

Preparation time: 15 mins
Cooking time: 10 mins

6 small salmon steaks
30ml (2 tablespoons) olive oil

15ml (1 tablespoon) freshly chopped coriander

For the sauce

1 medium onion, chopped
3 large peaches, skinned and chopped, discarding central stone

10ml (2 teaspoons) grated root ginger
15ml (1 tablespoon) clear honey
60ml (4 tablespoons) dry cider

To garnish
spring onion curls

radish roses

1. Make the sauce. Put the onion into a medium-sized pan with the peaches, ginger, honey and cider.
2. Bring to the boil, then simmer uncovered for 10 minutes until pulpy.
3. Process in the blender until smooth. Serve warm or cold.

4. Cook the salmon. Arrange salmon on lightly oiled grill rack. Brush over with oil. Sprinkle with coriander.
5. Grill for 3 minutes. Turn each steak over and grill for a further 3 minutes, until cooked. Set aside to cool.
6. Carefully peel skin away from salmon and divide each steak into two, discarding central bone.
7. Arrange salmon on serving dish and serve garnished with spring onion curls and radish roses and accompanied by the peach sauce.

Wedding Buffet

Serves 20

A very special cold buffet menu that's easy to prepare. Serve a selection of wines, beers and fruit juices.

Menu

Seafood Platter with Tomato Salsa Sauce (*see page 128*)
Tomato, Chive & Celery Salad
Country Salad
Special Rice Pilau (serve cold) (*see page 68*)
Spinach & Cheese Terrine
Brandied Chicken

~ ● ~

Basket of assorted bread rolls & butter

~ ● ~

Summer Fruit Salad with single cream
Two Autumn Puddings with Greek Yoghurt (*see page 142*)

Order

1. Prepare the spinach and cheese terrines, the tomato salsa sauce, the brandied turkey and two autumn puddings the day before the party. Prepare three times the recipe for special rice pilau, but do not add pistachio nuts until ready to serve. Cover each dish, once completely cold, and chill in refrigerator until ready to serve.
2. On the day, prepare the fruit salad early on. Cover and chill until ready to serve.
3. Prepare the tomato, chive and celery salad and the country mixed salad up to 1½ hours before you want to serve. Chill, adding dressing on serving.

4. About 20 minutes before serving, arrange the spinach and cheese terrines on a serving dish. Garnish and serve. Then serve brandied chicken and garnish. Add nuts to pilau rice and serve. Dress salads and serve.
5. Prepare and serve seafood platter and salsa sauce.

Seafood Platter
Serves 10

You will need two of these platters to serve 20 guests, so double the quantities given below.

Preparation time: 15 mins
Cooking time: approx. 6 mins

For the fish

5 × 175g (6oz) fresh salmon
   steaks
Salt and freshly ground black
   pepper
225g (8oz) smoked salmon,
   sliced and rolled
10 fresh oysters (frozen are
   easiest to open)

450g (1lb) peeled large prawns,
   defrosted if frozen
20 cooked mussels, in their
   shells
10 large, cooked prawns, in
   their shells
Juice of 1 lemon

To garnish

2–3 handfuls of fresh herbs,
   such as basil, parsley,
   tarragon, celery leaves,
   roughly chopped

Few nasturtium flowers
Few Little Gem lettuce leaves

To serve

wedges of 2 lemons

yoghurt mayonnaise (see page
   131)

1. Arrange the herbs, nasturtium flowers and lettuce leaves attractively on a large oval platter.

2. Grill the salmon steaks, seasoned with a little salt and pepper, under a medium heat for about 6 minutes until just cooked, turning each steak over halfway through cooking time. Allow to cool, then split each steak in half lengthways, discarding skin and central bone.
3. Arrange fish in groups according to kind, on the herbs (keep peeled prawns in a dish in centre).
4. Sprinkle lemon juice over and serve garnished with the wedges of lemon, accompanied by the yoghurt mayonnaise.

Tomato, Chive & Celery Salad

Preparation time: 20 mins
Cooking time: 0

1.5kg (3lb) baby tomatoes
1 head celery

1 1/2 yellow peppers
1 bunch chives

For the dressing

250ml (8 fl oz) olive oil
120ml (4 fl oz) red wine vinegar
15ml (1 tablespoon) dried basil
2 cloves garlic, crushed

Salt and freshly ground black pepper
Pinch mustard powder
2.5ml (1/2 teaspoon) brown sugar

1. Halve the tomatoes and put into serving dishes.
2. Chop the celery and chop and seed the peppers and add to the bowls.
3. Snip the chives into the dishes.
4. Prepare the dressing. Put all ingredients into a mixing bowl and whisk with a fork.
5. Pour dressing over salad. Toss to coat. Set aside for 10 minutes for flavours to mingle, then serve.

Country Salad

Preparation time: 20 mins
Cooking time: 0

1 large Iceberg lettuce
2 oak leaf lettuces
2 × 300g (11oz) bags rocket
1 bag ready-washed watercress

2 handfuls of freshly chopped herbs and a few pretty edible flowers, such as coriander, chives, dill, parsley, celery leaves, borage flowers and nasturtium flowers

For the dressing

150ml (5 fl oz) sunflower oil
150ml (5 fl oz) walnut oil
120ml (4 fl oz) white wine vinegar
2 garlic cloves, crushed

15ml (1 tablespoon) granary mustard
Salt and freshly ground black pepper

1. Tear the washed lettuces into bite-sized pieces. Put them into large serving bowls with the other salad ingredients, except the flowers, and toss them together.
2. In a mixing bowl, mix dressing ingredients, blending them with a fork or balloon whisk. Taste dressing, adding more seasoning if necessary.
3. Pour dressing over salad just before serving and toss to coat. Add the flowers.

Spinach & Cheese Terrine

The terrine looks very pretty garnished with a few slices of the roasted garlic peppers (see page 201), used cold, of course. You will need a 1kg (2lb) loaf tin.

Preparation time: 20 mins
Cooking time: 0

Sunflower oil, for greasing
1 × 200g (7oz) bag fresh
  spinach leaves, well washed
450g (1lb) reduced fat cream
  cheese
450g (1lb) ricotta cheese
30ml (2 tablespoons) freshly
  chopped mixed herbs
  (parsley, dill, oregano,
  chives)

60ml (4 tablespoons) mango
  chutney
5ml (1 teaspoon) paprika
  pepper
Grated rind of 1 large orange
Juice of 1/2 orange
2 × 340g (12oz) cans
  sweetcorn kernels with
  peppers, drained

1. Lightly oil a 1kg (2lb) loaf tin and line with cling film.
2. Cook the spinach briefly in a little boiling water, until wilted
   (2 minutes). Rinse under cold water, then blot dry with
   absorbent kitchen paper.
3. Use the spinach to line base and sides of the tin, overlapping
   sides.
4. Beat cheeses together in a large bowl, until smooth. Add the
   herbs, chutney, paprika and orange rind and juice. Beat
   again, just to blend.
5. Spread half the cheese mixture into base of prepared tin.
6. Top evenly with the sweetcorn.
7. Spread remaining cheese mixture over the sweetcorn. Fold
   spinach over the loaf.
8. Refrigerate for 2 hours or overnight.
9. To serve, turn the terrine onto flat serving dish. Remove cling
   film and serve in thin slices.

Brandied Chicken

If cooked chicken breast meat is not available, raw chicken
breast fillet can be cut into dice and simmered in chicken stock
for about 5 minutes, until tender. Cook the chicken in two large
pans. Remove using a draining spoon and allow to cool.

Preparation time: 30 mins
Cooking time: 5 mins, if using raw chicken

75g (3oz) butter
10ml (2 teaspoons) mild curry
  powder
3 large onions, chopped
3 large red peppers, seeded and
  chopped
4 sticks celery, diced
2.75kg (6lb) cooked chicken
  breast fillets

450g (1lb) seedless black
  grapes
60ml (4 tablespoons) brandy
2 × 500ml (17 fl oz) jars good
  quality mayonnaise
30ml (2 tablespoons) freshly
  chopped tarragon

To serve
a bed of mixed salad leaves,
  rocket, watercress, baby cos,
  Little Gem, oak leaf

100g (4oz) toasted flaked
  almonds
paprika pepper

1. Melt the butter in a large frying pan. Stir in the curry powder,
   then add the onions, peppers and celery.
2. Sauté for about 10 minutes, until onions soften.
3. Divide contents of pan between two large mixing bowls. Add
   chicken to each bowl. Stir, then set aside to cool for 10
   minutes.
4. Add the grapes and brandy to the bowls, then the mayonnaise
   and tarragon.
5. Toss well to coat. Cover and chill until ready to serve.
6. To serve, divide the well washed and drained salad leaves
   between two large oval platters. Top with the brandied
   chicken mixture.
7. Sprinkle nuts and a dusting of paprika over each dish on
   serving.

Summer Fruit Salad

Preparation time: 20 mins
Cooking time: 0

*Approx. 2.25kg (5lb) mixed
fresh fruit, such as prepared
melon, plums, mangoes,
strawberries, redcurrants,
pink grapefruit, nectarines,
peaches, loganberries,
raspberries, oranges*

*300ml (10 fl oz) fresh orange
juice*
*90ml (6 tablespoons)
Cointreau*

To decorate
tiny sprigs of fresh mint

To serve
pouring cream

1. Wash and prepare the fruit, according to type. Cut into bite-sized pieces, holding the fruit over a bowl as you work to catch any juices.
2. Put the prepared fruit into one or two large serving bowls.
3. Divide the orange juice and Cointreau between the bowls. Stir gently to mix. Cover and chill until ready to serve.
4. On serving, decorate the fruit with sprigs of mint and serve with cream.

Index